Lessons from Desiderata

Psychological Perspectives on
a Poem by Max Ehrmann

Michael Slavit Ph.D.
psychologist

ISBN: 1502882639
ISBN 13: 9781502882639
Library of Congress Control Number: 2014921460
CreateSpace Independent Publishing Platform
North Charleston, South Carolina

Acknowledgements

To my parents, Irma and Leonard Slavit, for their love and support.

To my sister Betsy for her love, support and skilled editing assistance.

To my sister Bobbie for her love and support.

To Dr. David J. Drum for years of guidance and assistance.

To Thomas DiSanto for support and technical assistance.

Desiderata

Go placidly amid the noise and the haste
And remember what peace there may be in silence.
As far as possible, without surrender
Be on good terms with all persons.

Speak your truth quietly and clearly, and listen to others,
Even to the dull and the ignorant.
They, too, have their story.

Avoid loud and aggressive persons
They are vexatious to the spirit.
If you compare yourself to others
You may become vain or bitter,
For always there will be greater and lesser persons than yourself.

Enjoy your achievements as well as your plans.
Keep interested in your own career, however humble.
It is a real possession in the changing fortunes of time.

Exercise caution in your business affairs,
For the world is full of trickery.
But let this not blind you to what virtue there is.

Many persons strive for high ideals,
And everywhere life is full of heroism.

Be yourself. Especially do not feign affection.
Neither be skeptical about love,
For in the face of all aridity and disenchantment
It is as perennial as the grass.

Take kindly the counsel of the years,
gracefully surrendering the things of youth.

Nurture strength of spirit to shield you
against sudden misfortune.
But do not distress yourself with dark imaginings.
Many fears are born of fatigue and loneliness.

Beyond a wholesome discipline, be gentle with yourself.
You are a child of the Universe,
no less than the trees and the stars.
You have a right to be here.

And, whether or not it is clear to you
No doubt the Universe is unfolding as it should.
Therefore be at peace with your God
Whatever you conceive him to be.

And whatever your labors and aspirations
In the noisy confusion of life,
Keep peace in your soul.
With all its sham, drudgery and broken dreams,
It is still a beautiful world.
Be cheerful. Strive to be happy.

Introduction

In Latin, *desideratum* means "something to be desired." *Desiderata* is simply the plural form, thus meaning "things desired." Max Ehrmann was a writer from Terre Haute, Indiana. He studied law and then, after practicing law for a few years, he worked in a family business until about age forty. From that point on he devoted himself to his first love: writing. He wrote Desiderata between 1906 and 1920, copyrighting it in 1927. The poem appears to have gone unnoticed for over thirty years.

In 1959, the Reverend Frederick Kates was compiling inspirational works for The Old Saint Paul's Church in Baltimore, Maryland. He included the poem among his collection. A myth arose about the origins of the poem. The growth of the myth accelerated in 1965, when a copy of it was found at the bedside of the deceased Democratic statesman Adlai Stevenson. As the title is Latin and the poem's language is reminiscent of earlier poetic form, some persons believed the poem to be centuries old.

It has now been established that Max Ehrmann did in fact write the poem. It has been published in numerous magazines, newspapers, anthologies, posters and websites, and is now considered to be in the public domain. The poem offers a positive and gentle philosophy of life, and is beautifully written. The poem consists of a series of expressions of encouragement, or entreaties, about living well and at peace with the world. Nonetheless, many of Ehrmann's entreaties, however eloquent, are general, and are sweeping in their scope. I believe they need considerable explanation to be useful, in a practical way, as a guide to creating a more positive consciousness and a happier life.

As an example, consider the line "Go placidly through the noise and the haste." This is an excellent idea, but you may well ask, "How?" In this book, I will make specific suggestions on how to "go placidly," using both physical relaxation and metaphor. Another example is the line, "Nurture strength of spirit to shield you against sudden misfortune." This is a beautiful and elegant line. However, it raises the questions of what strength of spirit is, and of how to attain it. In this volume, I will offer ideas on how to develop ways of thinking that may be seen as "nurturing strength of spirit." I do not in any way offer these comments as a criticism of Max Ehrmann's work. I love his poem, and feel that Ehrmann did a wonderful job as a poet. I offer this book as my attempt to do my job as a psychologist, by expanding on Ehrmann's beautiful words in such a way as to render them an even more useful way of increasing peace and happiness. This book is **not an interpretation** of Max Ehrmann's poem, but rather a compilation of ideas on how to put his ideas into use in your everyday life.

OFFERING ONE

Go Placidly Amid the Noise and the Haste

• • •

This line obviously acknowledges that the world can be fast-paced and noisy, and encourages us to find a way to maintain a sense of peace while navigating our way through it. I will offer two means of maintaining that sense of peace and tranquility: metaphor and physical relaxation.

Metaphor

A metaphor is a literary device by which one idea, concept or situation is represented by an idea, concept or situation that, though different, has some common characteristic. For instance, you could say, "Life is a journey through rocky terrain." This is not literally true. You may live in a city, work indoors, and rarely see a rock. However, the occupational, financial and social realities of life may very well feel to you like rocky terrain in that they require attention, careful planning and hard work to navigate. Rocky terrain and life have a common characteristic: they require attention, careful planning and hard work. Thus, though the statement "Life is a journey through rocky terrain" is not literally true, it is nonetheless metaphorically true.

It is a common saying that a picture is worth a thousand words. Moreover, if that picture is one that you create in imagination, it is worth far more. This is especially true if the picture you create in your imagination is more than a mere picture, but is an image, made stronger and more vivid by use of your senses of sight, hearing and feeling. You could undoubtedly create many images of "going placidly amid the noise and the haste." I will suggest two.

The Lilly Pad

Have you ever seen lily pads floating on a pond? They are fragile bits of vegetable matter, but they can maintain themselves without breaking. If you have ever seen waves or ripples disturbing lily pads, you may remember how they manage this. They do not resist the waves or ripples. Rather, they conform to them. When the crest of a wave reaches the leading edge of the lily pad, that leading edge lifts up with the wave. You can then see the wave travel the length of the lily pad, as it yields to the wave beneath it. The lily pads ripple along with the water beneath them. In a sense, the lily pad rises above the rippling water beneath it. If you think of yourself as a lily pad, perhaps you can also rise above the noise and haste of your environment. This may leave you as undisturbed by the noise and the haste of life as the lily pad is by the ripple. You may use your senses of sight and feeling to make this image vivid and powerful for you.

The way you would shed rain from an umbrella

Another metaphor you may use to "go placidly amid the noise and the haste" is to imagine the noise and haste as rain. Imagine that you have the ability to maintain your own peacefulness by treating the noise and haste as you would treat the rain you would shed from an umbrella.

There is a way to make this metaphor even more powerful. I am sure you have seen people running to or from their cars on a rainy, windy day. Think carefully about how they behaved. You may recall that each time a gust of wind hit them, they would duck or flinch. Have you ever thought of how useless that behavior is? They have already been hit by the gust of wind; there is no way to undo that. Are they trying to prepare for the next gust? As we cannot see gusts of wind coming, that is nonsensical. However, it certainly does make us overly tense and agitated to try to duck and flinch in response to a rainy gust of wind. With the exceptions of large hailstones, or debris from a nearby tornado, there is little to fear from a gust of rain and wind. The next time you are going from place to place in the rain and wind, try something different. Let go and relax, paying particular attention to allowing your shoulders to drop down and relax. Walk normally and at a moderate pace, and recognize that you will not become any more wet or disheveled by walking placidly than you would by ducking and flinching. Practice this method every time you have an opportunity. When you have discovered how much better this feels, you will be able to use the umbrella metaphor even more effectively as a means to "go placidly amid the noise and the haste."

• • •

Physical Relaxation

Another way to go placidly is to learn to be deeply physically relaxed. The method I will describe for you is called progressive relaxation. This method has been around, as far as the western world is concerned, since the early part of last century, when a physiologist named Edmund Jacobson devised it. Jacobson was a physiologist who worked at places like Harvard, Cornell and Bell Laboratories. He was interested in what happens to people physically and medically when they say that they are nervous, tense and worked up. He and researchers since him have found some very interesting things. Every major system of the body is affected. The muscular-skeletal system is affected in that individual muscle fibers are shorter and tighter. Because those individual muscle fibers are shorter and tighter, there is increased activity in the nervous tissue that serves those muscles, so the nervous system is affected. Because those individual muscle fibers are shorter and tighter, the muscles want more oxygen, so the respiratory system is affected. The oxygen is delivered to the muscles through the bloodstream, so the circulatory system is affected. There is an increase in both blood pressure and heart rate. The endocrine system is affected, with an increased secretion of adrenaline into the bloodstream that, by the way, is a primary feature of a panic attack. The digestive system is affected, with an increased secretion of digestive acids. The integumentary system, which most of us call the skin, is affected in that there is an increase in skin conductance. Some people get rashes like hives or eczema when they are tense. Even the immune system is affected. T-lymphocyte cells fight infection, recruit B-cells to further fight infection, and induce a cascade of reactions on the part of the human immune system. However, these immune system reactions are less active and less available when we are tense. In summary, every major system of the body is affected by physical tension.

First, we set aside fifteen minutes, and we find a place in which can be comfortable and in which we will be undisturbed for fifteen minutes. The very process of ensuring that we will be undisturbed can pay dividends. I have had adults tell me that insisting on fifteen minutes of undisturbed time changed the dynamics in their homes. Their children had to adjust to the fact that they were not the Centre of the Universe one hundred percent of the time, and that that Mom or Dad has needs and rights, too. All by itself, insisting on the time to practice relaxation is an exercise in reducing distractions and behaving more purposefully.

Progressive relaxation is such a fine technique that even a mediocre practice of it can have a desirable effect. However, I recommend having a well-refined, excellent way of practicing the technique. When we are first learning it, the technique takes about fifteen minutes. Jacobson wanted to find one of those physical changes that could come under some voluntary control, so he chose the shortening of muscle fibers. In order to lengthen the muscle fibers and to induce an array of other reactions, we first tense, and then release, muscles throughout the body.

Find a comfortable position in which to perform your relaxation exercise. If you lie down on a sofa or a bed, ensure that your back, neck and head are in a comfortably aligned position. If you are seated in a chair, make sure your feet can rest flat on the floor and that your hands and arms are well supported. Your next preparation for the exercise is to take a few slow, deep breaths, exhaling naturally. You want your abdomen to rise and fall with each breath. When your abdomen rises with an inhalation, your diaphragm descends, and your lungs can fill more fully. If you are not sure you are breathing in this way, place the palm of one hand on your abdomen and take a few breaths. Some people suck in their stomachs and expand their chests when they breathe. That is not as relaxing a way to breathe, and does not allow the lungs to fill as well with air. If you are in fact breathing that way, take a few moments to practice deep breathing with your abdomen rising as you exhale.

You are now ready to go through the body, one major muscle group at a time. When you put tension in, do not use all your strength or anything like that. Just put in a moderate amount of tension. And when you let the tension go, let it go all at once. You will go through your body one muscle group at a time. You will put in moderate tension, and will let tension go all at once. You will be taking a few slow, deep breaths, focusing your attention in certain, special ways and enjoying your resulting relaxation.

Begin with a slow, deep breath . . . . . and, let go. Again, take a slow, deep breath. . . and let go. Make sure that you are allowing your abdomen to rise and fall with each breath. In our day-to-day lives we can become so involved with what is going on in our minds that we can totally lose touch with what is going on in our bodies. If you think about it, I am sure you will agree. Perhaps you can remember driving your car, and stopping for a break. Only at the break did you realize that you were driving all tensed up. Tension can build up without our even knowing it.

Now, remembering to use just a moderate amount of tension, make your right hand into a fist. Just be aware of what that tension is like, take a deep breath, and hold it . . . and, let go. Stretch your fingers out wide and, let them fall back into a natural, relaxed position. Your right hand may feel a little warm or tingly. Take a slow, deep breath. . . . and, let go.

Same hand . . . make your right hand into a fist, and straighten your right arm, putting tension all the way to your shoulder. Take a deep breath, and hold it . . . . . and, exhale and let go. Stretch the fingers wide, and let them relax. Pay careful attention to the difference between the tight, tense feeling and the relaxed feeling. The more aware we are of the difference between these feelings, the more easily we can let go . . . and the more fully we can relax. Take a slow, deep breath . . . and let go. Pause for a moment as you let yourself become fully aware of the difference between the tense feelings and the relaxed feelings. The next will be the last time for the right hand and the right arm. Make your right hand into a fist and straighten . . . moderate tension . . . hold it . . . and, exhale and let go. Stretch your fingers out wide . . . . . and, let them fall into a natural position. Let your imagination help. Imagine any remaining tension draining down your right arm and out through the fingertips of your right hand.

Already you have learned a good deal about how much tension you have to introduce in order for you to then fully appreciate, and fully enjoy, the feeling of relaxation. With that in mind, you will go to the left side. Do not introduce any more tension than you have to. Make your left hand into a fist. Put your mind and your awareness into that left hand and become fully acquainted with that tense feeling. Take a breath and hold it . . . and, exhale and let go. Stretch the fingers . . . and let them go.

With every muscle group that you work on you are going to feel more relaxed. With every muscle group you work on you are going to feel calmer.

Now make your left hand into a fist, and straighten your left arm. Introduce moderate tension all the way to the shoulder. Take a breath and hold it . . . and exhale and let go. Stretch the fingers, and let them go. Be aware of what it feels like as the tension that you put in fades away. Be aware of what it feels like as relaxation takes over. Now this will be the last time for the left hand and the left arm. Make your left hand into a fist and straighten . . . moderate tension . . . take a breath and hold it . . . and, exhale and let go.

Stretch the fingers . . . and let them relax. Notice the difference between tightness and relaxation. Just as with the right side, let your imagination help. Imagine any remaining tension draining down your left arm and out through the fingertips of your left hand.

Now draw your shoulders up as though you were going to pull them right up around your ears. Take a breath and hold it. Feel that tension . . . exhale, and let go. Let your shoulders enjoy the feeling that they are sinking down as deeply as they want to go. Let go a little more, and relax a little more. You will be surprised, and pleased, at how relaxed you can be. Make sure at this point that your hands and arms are in a comfortable, well-supported position.

In the muscles of the face you are going to introduce only a very small amount of tension – just enough for you to appreciate and enjoy the feeling of relaxation. We will start with the forehead. See if you can put a little tension in by gently knitting your eyebrows . . . and relax. Now gently raise your eyebrows . . . and relax. Feel what your forehead feels like as the tension that you put in fades away . . . and as relaxation takes over.

Now close your eyes and very slowly, very gradually, close your eyes a little bit tighter . . . and relax. You can allow your eyes to remain closed. Allow your forehead, your eyes, and your eyelids to all feel comfortable . . . perhaps a little heavy . . . and relaxed. Gently press your tongue against the roof of your mouth . . . and relax. Take a slow, deep breath . . . and . . . let go.

Place your teeth together in a good, firm, comfortable bite. Slowly, gradually, bite down a little harder, until you can feel some tension in your jaw . . . and . . . relax. As though you were very sleepy and had to yawn, open your mouth very wide like a big, wide yawn. And . . . relax. Allow your lips to remain a little bit apart, and feel what your face and your jaw feel like as the tension, and any tingling sensation that you introduced, fades away.

Straighten your right leg, bringing your heel off the floor. Draw your toes back, stretching your calf muscle . . . and relax. If you are sitting up, gently draw your right leg back just far enough for your foot to rest flat on the floor. Feel what your right leg feels like as the tension, and any tingling sensation that you introduced, fades away. Now straighten your left leg. Draw your toes back, stretching your calf muscle . . . and relax. Gently draw your left leg back, and feel what your left leg feels like as the tension, and any tingling sensation, fades away.

The last muscle group that you will add any tension to will be the abdomen. Take a breath and tighten your abdomen . . . hold it . . . and . . . exhale and let go. Continue to breathe normally. Be aware of what your abdomen feels like as it gently rises and falls with each breath. With every breath that you exhale, allow yourself to let go a little more. With every breath that you exhale, allow yourself to relax even more.

Think the following words: peaceful . . . calm . . . and serene. Imagine yourself saying those three words aloud . . . peaceful, calm and serene. You may find that you have a preference for one of the three. In your mind, select your favorite. And, in your mind only, without using your lips or your voice, think that word to yourself as you exhale. Do this for your next few breaths.

You have completed the tense/release portion of the relaxation exercise. The next instructions are for what I call "the focusing method." Draw your attention to your forehead and your eyes and let your forehead and eyes relax completely. Really let go throughout your forehead and eyes, and imagine the tiny muscles there becoming smooth and relaxed. Let your face and your jaw relax. Focus on a sense of stillness, like a pond without a ripple. Let your neck and your shoulders relax. Focus on a sense of letting go. And, as you let go throughout your neck and your shoulders, imagine the muscles there becoming smooth and relaxed. Let your right arm and your right hand relax, knowing, as you do now, that relaxation is a skill . . . knowing that you can acquire and then develop the skill of relaxation . . . knowing that in so doing you will be increasing your sense of self control . . . and knowing that increased self-control will improve your self confidence. Let your left arm and your left hand relax. Imagine any remaining tension draining down your left arm and out through the fingertips of your left hand. Let your entire upper body relax, including your shoulders, back and abdomen. Imagine tension leaving your body the way air might leave a deflating air mattress. Let the rest of your body relax, including your legs and your feet. As you each exhale each of your next few breaths, again, to yourself, repeat that word that you selected.

Imagine any remaining tension draining out of your muscles the way water might drain through a pipe, leaving your muscles smooth and relaxed. Let your shoulders feel they are sinking down as deeply as they want to go, leaving your hands and arms heavy and relaxed. Focus on a sense of letting go, leaving you with a sense of stillness, like a pond without a ripple.

Continue to relax for a few more moments, and tell yourself the following:

- At this moment you have no obligations other than to relax.
- In the week ahead you will retain a clear memory of the way you feel now, and even that memory will help you.
- Every time you practice relaxation you will succeed, and you will become more skilled with practice. If you relax before sleeping, you will sleep more peacefully and therefore, of course, you will awaken more refreshed.
- And, even more important, if you relax soon after rising, it will help you begin your waking period more relaxed. That will make you so much more aware of what tension feels like at its earliest noticeable onset, that you may be able to prevent its build-up in the first place. That will be a great accomplishment, and a savings of energy – energy that would otherwise be squandered in nervous tension.
- Something will happen this week . . . something that might ordinarily make you feel nervous or rattled. But you will feel less nervous than usual. You will deal with it. You will find a solution. You may even feel that you have shed a bit of unpleasantness from about you the way you would shed rain from an umbrella. And that will feel good.
- When you conclude the exercise and open your eyes, you will still feel relaxed, and you will also feel alert,

refreshed, and with a sense of well being. You will also be very much aware that you can develop your own internal skills to help yourself.

That concludes the progressive relaxation exercise. You may want to read the entire description as it is written on these pages before performing the exercise, and then to do the exercise by memory. A second method would be for you to read the transcript aloud and to record it for yourself. You would then be able to play it back for yourself as you perform the exercise. A third method would be to have another person read the instructions for you as you learn the technique. Regardless of which way you choose to acquire the skill of relaxation, you will find deep relaxation to be an enormous help in quieting your body and mind in such a way as to set the stage for more organized thought and actions. The next two pages are a brief review of the recommended use of the progressive relaxation method that has been presented.

Review of Progressive Relaxation

Since relaxation and anxiety are incompatible states, you can reduce anxiety by developing your ability to experience deep relaxation.

Set aside 15 minutes, and try to ensure you will be left undisturbed.

Sit comfortably in a chair, or recline, or lie down. If you sit up, place your feet flat on the floor and be sure your hands and arms are comfortably supported. If you are reclining or lying down, be sure your head, neck and back are comfortably aligned.

Experience the difference between tense and relaxed feelings by tensing and then relaxing muscles, as has been described. Introduce only as much tension as you need. After you have applied tension, take a breath and hold it for 3-5 seconds. Let go of tension all at once, as you exhale your breath. Do not hold your breath while working on the muscles of your face and head. Apply this procedure to your hands, hands and arms, shoulders, forehead, eyes, tongue, jaw, legs and abdomen.

After releasing tension, take a few moments to really feel and appreciate the difference between tense and relaxed feelings.

THE FOCUSING METHOD: Draw your attention to each muscle group again, one at a time. This time introduce no tension. Rather, just allow relaxation to deepen in one of the following ways:

- Imagine your muscles becoming smooth and relaxed.
- Imagine tension draining out of your muscles, like water through a pipe.
- Imagine tension leaving your body the way air might escape a deflating air mattress.
- Just focus on a sense of letting go.

Now and then, throughout the exercise, take a slow, deep breath and let it go. As you exhale, think your choice of the following three words: "peaceful, calm, or serene."

Practice these exercises three times per day. The purpose of these exercises is to build your skill of relaxation – not just to help soften a stress-filled week. Practice the exercise regardless of whether you are having an easy or a difficult week.

• • •

OFFERING TWO

And remember what peace there may be in silence

. . .

Do I have to contend that issue?

How many times in your life have you been drawn into debates or arguments about some social, political or other issue? Do you ever feel that these debates are tiresome, and drain you of energy? Have you ever noticed that the person or persons with whom you are debating stick to their point of view regardless of what you say? Do you ever find yourself, even in the midst of a debate, wondering why you are using your time and your energy in that manner?

Perhaps you could you ask yourself a question: "Is this the floor of the Senate or the House of Representatives?" If you are, in fact, a senator or congressional representative, then perhaps it is your duty to continue the debate. If not, then consider an alternative. You could just conclude that a) As you are not on the floor of congress, the debate is of limited use; b) You are unlikely to change your opponent's mind; and c) There may indeed be peace in silence.

Do I have to match the frenzy of my environment?

Max Ehrmann's phrase "the noise and the haste" probably does aptly describe many educational, work and social settings. It is natural for us to adapt to our environment. That adaptation may include increasing our state of arousal to match the energy level of our environment. We could either reduce our state of arousal to match a sedate setting or raise our state of arousal to match a high-energy setting. For instance, without any prompting or preparation, we assume a low-key demeanor in a library or while attending a funeral. Also without prompting or preparation, we are likely to be louder and more excitable at a sporting event or at a lively party.

But must it be so? Are we controlled by our environment, or can we monitor our own state of arousal and bring it to a level we choose instead of the level of the environment? For instance, you may find yourself among persons who are talking in an excited way about a topic in which you have very little interest. Or, you may be among people who are behaving in a frenzied or excited way when you are not feeling the same energy state. Despite your minimal interest, you may find yourself being dragged into the atmosphere of the situation. This might be an instance in which you would prefer to find peace in silence. Recall the use of metaphors suggested in the previous section concerning "going placidly amid the noise and the haste." We considered behaving the way a lily pad behaves when a ripple passes through it. And we considered the idea of walking in a relaxed manner and at moderate pace despite rain and wind. You may want to use such a metaphor to allow the noise and haste of the high-energy or frenzied setting to pass through you without disturbing you and without dragging you into that energy state. You may observe the situation, but find peace in silence.

• • •

OFFERING THREE

As Far as possible, without surrender, be on good terms with all persons

• • •

The encouragement to be on terms with all persons as far as possible requires no explanation. However, Ehrmann also includes the phrase "without surrender," and therein lies a potential problem. First, we need to think about what it is that we consider so valuable that we do not want to surrender it. Secondly, we need to consider the conditions under which we would refuse to surrender it. It can be argued that there is a multitude of things we might not want to surrender, but I will discuss three: dignity, closely held values or beliefs, and resources.

Surrender of Dignity

Dignity can be described as the state or quality of being worthy of honor or respect. It can also be described as self-respect attained by maintenance of our independence, boundaries and rights. In the comings and goings of our work lives, social lives, family lives and consumer lives, there are many ways in which the world can impinge on our dignity. And, if you really consider it, you will realize that in each instance of an intrusion on your dignity, you implement a decision. You decide whether you are willing to accept an intrusion, and you decide on an acceptable degree of that intrusion.

Let us consider our work and financial lives. The degree of intrusion we are willing to accept is very much dependent on our life circumstances. If you are skilled in a profession in which there is high demand for your services, and if your material and financial life is in order, you may decide to accept very little in the way of an intrusion on your dignity. If your boss were to come in and tell you that you have to start punching a time clock, and that you must now ask permission to take your lunch break, you may decide that these demands represent an unacceptable intrusion on your dignity. You might then inform your boss that you will leave if those requirements are not immediately withdrawn. However, suppose your situation in life is not as strong. If you feel fortunate to have your job and are having difficulty meeting your financial responsibilities, you may find yourself accepting such an intrusion. In poet Ehrmann's terms, you might have to "surrender" in order to remain on good terms with someone.

My daughter is a college student, and she was working at a restaurant as a server and bartender. One day her boss swore at her for no good reason. She looked him in the eye, took off her apron, and left. She has the support of her parents and was fortunate to be in a position to defend, rather than surrender, her dignity. Of course, I told her I was very proud of her for not allowing herself to be treated that way. However, not everyone is in a position to defend his or her dignity as fiercely.

Surrender of closely held values or beliefs

I was socializing with some friends in a state park on one occasion, and a friend of mine dropped some litter on the ground. I place a high value on avoiding littering. However, I did not feel there was any need to chide my friend about his dropping litter on the ground. In this instance, I felt that I would lessen my good terms with my friend by criticizing or correcting him, and in the service of being on good terms, I let my value of avoidance of litter slide.

On another occasion, I was with a friend in the parking lot near a hike and bike trail. We saw a couple of young women drive right in and park in a "handicapped only" spot, despite there being many regular parking spaces available. I said I was going to speak to the two women about their inconsideration. My friend asked me not to, saying things such as "Don't make a scene," and "Just let it alone." It was obvious that my friend would be disappointed in me if I were to speak to the two young women. However, I hold the value of consideration very highly, and I went and spoke with the women, asking them to move their car out of the "handicapped only" spot. In this instance, I decided to uphold the value of consideration. Speaking up in opposition to intrusive, thoughtless behavior was so important to me that I was not willing to surrender that value to stay on good terms with my friend.

You undoubtedly find yourself in similar situations. There are sure to be times when your desire to stay on good terms with someone, and your desire to remain true to your values or beliefs, will be in conflict. For instance, imagine that you are interviewing for a job, and the interviewer says something you find socially or politically offensive. You will have to make a quick decision as to whether to defend your value or belief, or to stay on good terms with the interviewer.

Surrender of resources

I had a patient who had a number of misfortunes in her life. To give her a name I will call her "Jane." Jane's misadventures had left her without any financial savings, and she had a modest monthly income. Jane was a divorced woman in her mid-forties, and her opportunities to secure her financial future were very limited. Her daughter (I will call her Kim) was in her mid-twenties, married, and with one child. Kim's husband, though capable of work, was not working. Kim and her husband liked to order take-out food instead of saving money by buying their food in a market and doing their own cooking. Jane was paying their monthly cell phone bill, and was giving them money at other times as well. It was obvious that Jane was so afraid to lose her "good terms" with her daughter and son-in-law that she was willing to surrender a significant portion of her very modest financial resources. From my point of view, I felt that a woman in her mid-twenties, with a husband capable of work, had much more time and opportunity to secure her financial future than did a divorced woman in her mid-forties. To me, it seemed as though Kim was being extremely intrusive and self-centered to believe that it was okay to spend extra money to avoid cooking, and to expect her less resourceful mother to pay some of her bills. Poet Ehrmann's advice is to be on good terms with others, as far as possible, without surrender. I believe that Jane was ignoring the "without surrender" part of this advice. Her surrender of resources may very well have been inappropriate under the circumstances.

On the other hand, there are sure to be instances in which it is desirable and appropriate to surrender resources in order to be on good terms with others. You may feel that this is especially true if the relationship in question is, or has potential to be, reciprocal. However, in some circumstances we may surrender resources simply because we wish to be a generous, giving person. Even if it is not reciprocal, surrendering resources to remain on good terms with others is appropriate if we judge the risk versus reward ratio to be favorable, or if we just feel like being a giving person in the particular situation.

We have considered the issue of surrender, specifically surrender of dignity, of closely held values or beliefs, and of resources. Max Ehrmann encourages us to be on good terms with all persons, but to do so without surrender. I hope we have explored the issue of surrender in sufficient detail. I hope that as a reader you will be able to use the ideas and examples provided to develop your own criteria. I hope you will develop a clear idea of when being on good terms with others is, or may not be, worth the risk of surrendering something you hold dear.

• • •

OFFERING FOUR

Speak your truth quietly

and clearly,

and listen to others,

even to the dull and the ignorant;

They too have their story.

• • •

The advice to speak our truth quietly and clearly appears to be a straightforward suggestion to express ourselves without undue vehemence or intensity. If we do add extra volume or intensity to what we say, we may succeed not in convincing others of our truth, but only in making the recipient resistant to our message.

Listening to others is very important for at least three reasons. First, if we fail to listen to others, we are denying ourselves access to a point of view of which we may be unaware. We may thus fail to add to our own knowledge and awareness. Secondly, failing to listen to others may cause us to appear aloof or arrogant. Third, we may impair the quality of our social relations simply by failing to comply with an implied social convention to listen as much as we speak.

Ehrmann goes on to add, "even to the dull and the ignorant; they too have their story." Many readers may have an initial reaction of wanting to avoid wasting their time listening to the dull and the ignorant. However, Ehrmann's words are worthy of consideration. First, until we listen to others, we do not have a basis on which to judge them ignorant. For instance, many persons have grown up in homes in which good language usage was absent. Others possess good intelligence but lack formal education. They may express intelligent ideas, but may use language that interferes with an appreciation of the quality of their thoughts. Some persons who on initial impression may appear dull or ignorant may turn out to be worth hearing if we allow ourselves to listen.

Even if, after listening, we still judge someone dull and ignorant, there may still be a virtue in listening. First, we may be enhancing our own humanity and our own generosity of spirit by listening. By listening, we are acknowledging that someone can be worthy as a human being even if we do not judge them to be sharp and knowledgeable. That acknowledgement may make us less judgmental persons. Being less judgmental may be seen as a more elevated way of being. Secondly, if we not only admit that "dull and the ignorant" persons have their story, but communicate back to them that we have heard that story, we have performed an act of kindness. Performing acts of kindness is another way of attaining a more elevated way of being.

• • •

OFFERING FIVE

Avoid loud and aggressive persons

They are vexatious to the spirit.

• • •

At first glance, this may seem to be entirely self-explanatory. There are times when individuals behave in loud or aggressive ways that are very obvious. Avoiding them whenever possible is a clear choice, and I do not believe I have to belabor that issue. However, people can be "vexatious to the spirit" in ways that are, albeit less obvious, destructive nevertheless. I am thinking in particular about behavior that, while not necessarily openly aggressive, is nonetheless aggressive due to being presumptuous. I hope I can be of better service to readers by exploring this concept.

Here are a few dictionary definitions of the verb to presume:

- to act or proceed with unwarranted or impertinent boldness;
- to go too far in taking liberties;
- to take something for granted.

Briefly, then, a presumptuous act is one in which a party takes unwarranted liberties and imposes something on another party. Here are a few illustrations:

One) Gary has his car, and offers a ride to Jonathan. Gary enters the highway and speeds up to 90 miles/hour, making some quick lane changes to get around other traffic. Jonathan asks Gary to slow down, but Gary replies, "Relax, we'll be fine."

(Gary is acting presumptuously by presuming it is acceptable to impose on Jonathan a risk to which Jonathan has not agreed).

Two) Jeffrey and Sandra are a married couple with a 2-year old son, Max. Sandra's parents, Martin and Phyllis, come for a visit. While they are sitting in the living room, Max reaches for Phyllis' pocketbook. Phyllis says, "Bad boy, Max," and gives his hand a gentle slap. Sandra says, "Mom, please don't do that again! We never tell Max he's 'bad,' and we don't ever slap him." Phyllis replies, "Don't be silly. We can't just let him reach for other people's belongings."

(It is up to Jeffrey and Sandra to decide how to bring up their child. Phyllis is presumptuous in believing she has a right to impose her methods on them).

Three) Two families have gone to a picnic grove near a brook. They are enjoying a picnic and are talking softly, enjoying the peace and quiet, and the sounds of nature. Two couples drive into the grove with their car stereo blasting. They get out of the car and leave the car doors open so their loud music fills the picnic grove.

(The arriving couples are presumptuous in thinking it is acceptable to change the conditions of the picnic grove that the families had been enjoying in peace and quiet).

Four) Mark asks Mike to join him for a hike. Mike later calls Mark and asks, "Were you just hoping for some one-on-one 'Mark and Mike time', or is it okay if I invite my girlfriend Debbie?" Mark says it is fine to bring her. Mike calls Debbie and describes the interaction he had with Mark, telling her she is invited on the hike. Debbie then calls her friend Claudia and invites her along.

(Mark is the originator of the hiking plans. It is "his party." Mike was considerate to ask Mark if Debbie could come along. Debbie was presumptuous in thinking she had a right to change the conditions of the hike without asking).

Five) Pete, Marie, Al and Rose are at a drive-in restaurant, eating sandwiches. They decide to order a large plate of French fries to share. Marie goes to get the fries and, before she returns, she finds a ketchup server and puts a generous amount of ketchup on the fries. When she returns, Al and Rose complain that they do not like ketchup on French fries.

(Marie was presumptuous in assuming she had a right to impose her preference for ketchup on the others).

The above examples all depict one party imposing some conditions on another, or others. They are clearly not all of the same degree of seriousness. In fact, we could probably rate them on a presumptuousness scale of 1 to 5, as follows:

1. Extreme – possibly catastrophic
2. Very intrusive - with possible long-term consequences
3. Moderate - intrusive, but relatively short-term
4. Relatively mild and short-term
5. Very mild and fleeting

Gary's subjecting Jonathan to highway risk is extreme. Phyllis's intrusion on Jeffrey and Sandra's parental rights is very intrusive. The couples changing the atmosphere of the picnic grove from serene to raucous is quite intrusive, but short-term. Debbie's inviting another hiker without consultation is relatively mild. And Marie's imposing ketchup on her dining partners' French fries is mild and fleeting. However, regardless of where they fall on the mild-to-extreme continuum, all these behaviors have something in common. They are presumptuous in that they change other people's reality without permission.

What can we do if others are presumptuous?

Assertive communication may be helpful. There is an assertive paradigm that, though rather stiff and formal, can help us to think through some important components of an assertive communication. The paradigm is as follows:

I see (or I hear) . . . I feel . . . I imagine . . . I want . . .
It might proceed like this:

I hear you telling Max he is a "bad boy,"
I feel intruded upon and annoyed,
I imagine you think you can impose your view of parenting on us, and
I want you to respect our views and methods for raising Max.

Though somewhat stiff and formal, this assertive paradigm has a few distinct advantages. First, it starts out with a simple description of what you see or hear – a factual description of the other party's behavior. Second, it informs the other party of your feelings in response to their behavior. Unless the other party is very callous, this helps them to understand the emotions they are imposing on others. Third, by using the words "I imagine," we avoid making our statement seem too judgmental. Fourth, we make a direct statement of what we want.

An alternative to this paradigm is to make a simple statement of what we want. For instance:

- Gary, I'm not telling you how to drive when I'm not in your car, but don't put me at risk when I am.
- Mom, it's not up to you to decide how Max is raised. You have to respect our methods.
- Listen, guys, we were enjoying this place in peace. I think you should turn off your stereo and not disturb the peace we were enjoying.
- Debbie, this was Mark's party. I asked him if I could invite you, and it would have been more courteous for you to ask if you could invite Claudia.
- Come on, Marie. From now on, ask if you can put condiments or seasonings on food that other people will share.

What can we do if we find we are being presumptuous?
Perhaps a good way to learn to be less presumptuous, or less intrusive on others, is to learn to increase our sense of empathy. It may be helpful to observe various interactions between and among people, and to imagine what we would feel like if we were one of the involved parties. If we suspect, or have been informed by someone else, that we are prone to being presumptuous, we may want to try to imagine the emotions people may feel in response to intrusive behavior. Following are lists of emotions arranged in two categories: intrusion/vulnerability and belittlement/inferiority.

INTRUSION / VULNERABILITY

beaten	caged	deprived
exhausted	hassled	helpless
intruded upon	invaded	overpowered

powerless	put upon	scorned
unprotected	used	vulnerable
weak		

BELITTLEMENT / INFERIORITY

abused	ashamed	belittled
criticized	defeated	demoralized
discounted	disgraced	embarrassed
humiliated	hurt	intimidated
mistreated	put down	ridiculed
slighted		

First, we would have to discipline ourselves to observe interactions among others, including interactions in which one party subjected another party to presumptuous or intrusive behavior. Then we would have to imagine, using the vocabulary listed above, how we might feel if we were the one being intruded upon. If we can truly imagine those feelings, then we are training ourselves to be more sensitive to those feelings. This could help us avoid behaving that way in the future.

A Final Note about Presumptuousness

Thoughtful, considerate behavior among people is a joy. Focusing on and displaying appreciation for thoughtful behavior is the best way to encourage it. However, there are times when we may feel the need to comment on or intervene in presumptuous behavior to set the stage for more considerate behavior to emerge.

• • •

OFFERING SIX

If you compare yourself to others

You may become vain or bitter

For always there will be greater

and lesser persons than yourself

. . .

Years ago I formulated fifteen principles for happiness, which are shown in Appendix A. Principle fifteen is as follows:

> Principle for Happiness FIFTEEN: Imagine a weight lifter, looking in the mirror and comparing himself to other weight lifters. The idea here has to do with comparisons. When we compare ourselves to others, we get one of two results. Either we judge ourselves to be superior and feel conceited or we judge ourselves to be inferior and feel deprived. Neither feeling will make us happy. Some comparisons are inevitable, but it will be in our better interest to limit them if we can.

I wrote that if we compare ourselves to others we will feel conceited or deprived, and Ehrmann wrote that we will feel vain or bitter. We are clearly on the same page. If we judge ourselves to be inferior, we will end up feeling bitter because we feel deprived. Ehrmann clearly used a more poetic and eloquent expression when he wrote, "For always there will be greater and lesser persons than yourself."

I think it is important to emphasize that the comparisons in question are overall comparisons of our totality, essence or worth as human beings. Later in this book I will be addressing Ehrmann's entreaty that we "Nurture strength of spirit." As part of that discussion, I will explore the idea that no one can judge the totality, essence or worth of another human being. If we can think deeply and often about that idea, hopefully we can convince ourselves at a deep level that it is true. Then, comparisons with others will not be threatening, since our worth as human beings will not be at issue.

When we are convinced that our worth is not at issue, there is no danger of becoming vain or bitter if we simply compare one or more of our skills or attributes to others. If we believe ourselves to be in better physical condition than someone else, or to be a better writer, singer, dancer or public speaker, we can take pride in our accomplishments without becoming vain. Moreover, if we find that someone else has more knowledge or skill in an area we value, we can ask for coaching or guidance without feeling deprived or bitter. We would not learn from a teacher or mentor if we did not first assume that our teacher has greater knowledge or skill in some area than we have.

Learning not to compare our totality, essence or worth to others allows us increased flexibility and comfort in life. It enables us to enjoy our achievements (another Ehrmann entreaty), successes and positive attributes without worrying about vanity or self-absorption. It allows us to seek help, guidance and knowledge from others without feeling inferior or deprived. It allows us to be more emotionally responsive to life with less emotional baggage.

• • •

OFFERING SEVEN

Enjoy your achievements as well as your plans

. . .

By suggesting that we enjoy our achievements, I believe Ehrmann is entreating us to live in the moment long enough to enjoy what we are doing, rather than to turn our attention too quickly to the future. He is asking us to stop long enough to savor the moment when we have achieved something. In addition, when considering the ideas of *Desiderata* as a whole, it is also implied that we can enjoy our achievements without becoming vain, as we realize that "always there will be greater and lesser persons than ourselves" (this was discussed in the last chapter).

Many people describe the experience of putting off relaxation, leisure and happiness for the present until some landmark event has passed. For instance, they say, "I'll slow down and relax after I graduate college." After graduation they say, "I'll slow down and relax after I am hired for my first professional job." After being hired they say, "I'll slow down and relax after I pass my probationary period at work." After that, it's

"I'll slow down after I buy a home," then "I'll slow down after I marry," then "I'll slow down after I have my first child," then "I'll slow down after my child graduates high school," et cetera. They describe the pattern of pushing to achieve the next milestone, but not slowing down to appreciate what they have done so far. They are always telling themselves they will enjoy and savor life "just around the next curve," or "just over the next rise." In Ehrmann's terms, they are focusing on their plans, but not enjoying their achievements.

Again I will refer you to one of my fifteen principles for happiness. Principle seven is as follows:

> Principle for Happiness SEVEN: If there is such a thing as heaven on Earth, it comes when we are fully aware that life is a process and not a product. Your life is not a resume … not a portfolio … not a house under construction. The expression "my life is ruined" is possible only when we feel life is a product instead of what it is in reality - a succession of moments for us to experience.

This is a very challenging set of ideas, and it requires a balance between apparently competing concepts. We can get lost while examining the terms "process versus product" and "achievements versus plans." I will try to be as clear as I can in illustrating this point. Although it is important to enjoy our achievements, we would not have managed any achievements without first having made plans. As an example, graduating college is an achievement, but we would not graduate had we not made plans to take the courses needed to meet the requirements for the degree. We may have wanted to enjoy the process of learning, but we would not graduate without seeing the degree as a product worth having.

We may need a balance between a process orientation and a product orientation to attain happiness and contentment. For instance, when autumn arrives, many individuals complain that summer "got away from them," and they did not enjoy many of the summer activities they had hoped to enjoy. At the beginning of summer, they thought the season would be long, and they did not feel a need to be organized and diligent about planning events. However, too relaxed an attitude about planning and organizing their summer resulted in their autumn disappointment.

One such individual – we will call him "Roy" – had this feeling more than once when autumn arrived. He finally made a mental list of ten activities. He wanted to enjoy the activities, and when autumn arrived, he wanted to be able to look back and know he had *not* missed his preferred summer pleasures. He made the following list:

1. Swimming at a surf beach
2. A day of sliding down the slides at a water park
3. A day of riding the rides at an amusement park
4. Attending a minor league baseball game
5. Celebrating the 4th of July
6. A day of bicycle riding on an island
7. Hosting a cookout
8. Golf
9. Kayaking
10. Sailing

Each time Roy took part in one of the ten activities, he would imagine putting a checkmark next to that item on his mental list. When autumn came, he would feel a sense of satisfaction if he had checked off most of the ten items. The first question, then, is whether Roy was engaging in a process orientation or a product orientation toward his summer. And the answer is both. The important questions are 1. What was the relative strength of his focus on process and product? and 2. What was the effect of this on his experience and happiness?

If Roy were truly enjoying the moment-to-moment experience of his preferred activities, and checking the activity off the list were merely a symbolic gesture, then we could say his process orientation is primary. If, however, he engaged in the activities without full attention and immersion, and if he were already thinking about the next activity to be checked off, then we could say his product orientation was primary. To illustrate this point more fully, consider an hypothetical example. Imagine it is late summer, and Roy has not yet gone bicycling on an island. Imagine there will be no more opportunities this summer, and he sets aside the last available day to engage in this activity. But when the day arrives, the weather is very unfavorable. Roy may let the bicycling go, and do something that he can enjoy even with the unfavorable weather. He may not worry about finishing the summer without the island bicycle ride. Again, we would say that he was primarily process oriented. On the other hand, Roy might be so intent on earning his checkmark that he might go to the island, have an uncomfortable ride in poor weather and attain his checkmark. In this case we could say that he had forgotten the original intent of his list, and that he had become too product oriented.

Balancing process and product in the conduct of our lives is a challenge. But it is that balance that can allow us, in poet Ehrmann's terms to "enjoy our achievements as well as our plans."

• • •

OFFERING EIGHT

Keep interested in your own

career, however humble.

It is a real possession

in the changing fortunes of time.

· · ·

When Sigmund Freud was asked what he believed makes an emotionally well-adjusted person, he replied, "To love and to work." I also believe that feeling purposeful is a very important component of a happy existence. I often use the following words, almost as a mantra: "a place to go, people to see and a function to perform." It is important to recall that it was somewhere between 1906 and 1920 when Max Ehrmann entreated us to keep interested in our career, "however humble." In the early decades of the twentieth century, it was common for families to get by with one wage earner. Economic realities were quite different then compared to today. For instance, the cost of housing as a percentage of family income was much lower then. What Ehrmann would have considered a "humble career" might not be as rewarding today.

Nonetheless, there is much to be said for being active, purposeful and in motion as opposed to lacking a sense of purpose and of feeling immobilized. Even if economic conditions or our own finances are not going well, it is better to keep interested in our work. If we fail to do that, we run the risk of feeling immobilized which, as I have seen in the cases of many patients, can lead to loss of self-esteem and to depression. When life feels like a struggle, avoiding immobilization is very important. If your occupation feels unrewarding or "humble," keep at it and strive to find a better situation. The very process of getting yourself "up and out," and of at least earning something to try to meet your financial needs, will be far better for your energy level and your psychological well-being than being immobilized. In Ehrmann's words, our occupation truly is "a real possession in the changing fortunes of time."

I would like to add another thought to this discussion. I have on a number of occasions worked with patients who found themselves experiencing a sense of dread about going to work. I am not referring to situations in which there was a genuine threat. Sometimes a person will develop a sense of dread, and a desire to avoid work, even in the absence of any specific indignity or threat.

If you are eighty-five years of age, please do not be offended by my following remarks. There are times when a comparison between conditions or stages of life may seem disrespectful to a person at that stage or in that condition. I apologize for that, but sometimes such a comparison is useful to an individual. To a young or middle-aged worker who has come to dread getting up ad going to work, I have sometimes said something like the following:

> At this stage of your life, you have developed an aversion to getting up, getting out, and slugging it out with

the world of work. That is understandable. However, I would like you to consider the following. Project yourself into the future. Imagine that you are eighty-five years old. Imagine yourself getting up in the morning. Imagine that your muscles are stiff, and that it takes you an hour, and a heating pad, to be loosened up enough to move around normally. Imagine that you are aware that outside your home, the hustle and bustle of life is going on without you. You have leisure time, but you may lack a sense of purpose. Can you imagine what you might be thinking? Can you imagine that you might be thinking something like this: "Here I am, without enough energy to get out there and slug it out with the world of work. I know it is not all fun and games out there, but the people who are out there are part of the pulse of daily life. I just wish, when I was younger, that I had been more grateful for having had the ability to leave home and take part in the world of work."

If you can imagine the possibility of feeling that way, perhaps you can help yourself to appreciate what you have. Perhaps you can appreciate your career, however humble, simply because you are able to do it.

• • •

OFFERING NINE

Exercise caution in your

business affairs,

For the world is full of trickery.

But let this not blind you to what

virtue there is.

Many persons strive

for high ideals,

and everywhere life is full

of heroism.

• • •

Ehrmann is encouraging us to strive for balance between skepticism on the one hand and faith in our fellow human beings on the other. Exercising caution in our business affairs has become axiomatic in our society. We have expressions such as "caveat emptor" (Let the buyer beware) and "When you snooze, you lose." Personally, I deplore those expressions. I think it is tragic that winning financially in a transaction has reached a higher level of value than conducting ourselves with integrity. Nonetheless, many individuals and financial institutions are motivated more by greed and opportunism than by devotion to honesty and integrity.

What are we to do? In Ehrmann's words, we are to exercise caution, while not letting our caution "blind us to what virtue there is." How do we attain this balance? We may attain it with vigilance, and with great difficulty. Of course, we have resources that did not exist in Ehrmann's time to help us to be cautious. We have better business bureaus, we have departments of business regulation and we have a plethora of Internet on-line services to help us in this regard. However, we still have the problem that persons attempting to sell us goods and services may be skilled at creating an image of honesty even if their intent is to take advantage of us.

While it is in our better interest to invest some energy in learning to protect ourselves from financial exploitation, our happiness probably requires that even more energy be allocated to appreciating virtue. From the point of view of our emotional lives, we serve ourselves better by focusing on and appreciating the good will shown by persons of good faith than by focusing on the ill will of dishonest or overly opportunistic persons.

In addition, if we conduct ourselves with reason and fairness, we are exerting some influence on the world. I am sure you can recall being treated with fairness and honesty in a business transaction, and having your sense of good will from that transaction carry over to your next encounter. Simply put, if we are too aggressive in business with others, they will feel embittered and will be aggressive in their next transaction. But if we are fair and reasonable in our dealings with others, they are at least somewhat more likely to feel a sense of good will and to be fair and honest in their next encounter. Fairness and good will can be infectious, as can be their less desirable counterparts. Ehrmann encourages us to exercise caution, but to be open to virtue as well. Our caution can protect us, but it is our openness to virtue that can exert a positive influence on those around us.

• • •

OFFERING TEN

Be yourself. Especially do not feign affection.

• • •

O ne obvious interpretation of these words is: Do not pretend to be in romantic love. It is deceptive and hurtful to string someone along romantically. Feigning affection in that way is clearly out of bounds if we are striving to live an elevated, ethical life.

However, I believe there is a more prevalent, and perhaps even more destructive, way in which people tend to feign affection. I am referring to the outward respect people often show to persons whom they do not truly respect. I will describe an hypothetical example and you, gentle reader, can search your memories to see if you have ever had any experiences such as this. Imagine a company, agency, or a school, in which a manager or administrator misuses his power. Rather than referring to this hypothetical person as "that manager or administrator," I will just use a common name - Doug. And I will use the word "agency" instead of writing "agency, company or school." Imagine that in his position Doug has great influence over the working conditions and career opportunities of many other persons. Imagine that Doug misuses his power in a number of ways. Perhaps Doug displays favoritism toward some employees over others. Perhaps he seems callous to the needs of employees to have comfortable working conditions. Perhaps Doug is aloof, and rejects reasonable suggestions or input from his staff. Perhaps he is dishonest. Imagine that virtually everyone in the agency recognizes Doug's failings. And yet, imagine that almost everyone in the agency treats Doug with outward respect. Imagine that staff members typically greet Doug pleasantly, try to exchange some pleasantries and, in general, "play up to him."

You may ask, "What is the harm in being pleasant?" The harm is that if everyone is pleasant and civil toward Doug, then there is no natural consequence brought to bear on him for his favoritism, callousness, aloofness and dishonesty. He will go on doing what he is doing, and agency employees, and probably the agency itself, will suffer. By continuing to be pleasant toward Doug – by "feigning affection" as it were – staff members fail to give Doug a message that his behavior and attitude need improvement.

At this point, you may ask, "Would it be better to be insulting or to be uncivil?" No, the alternative to feigning affection is not to be uncivil or insulting. A cool or detached attitude might be a start. But the real answer is assertive communication. For instance, if an employee has brought suggestions to Doug on how to improve the agency's efficiency, only to be rejected each time, that employee might want to communicate assertively as follows: "Doug, I hear you rejecting my suggestion, as you have done before. I am frustrated that you do not recognize my creativity and dedication to the agency. I imagine you believe you can run the agency without respecting input and without concern for staff morale. And I want you to recognize the importance of teamwork and to reconsider my suggestion." If only one individual were to communicate in this way, there is not much chance for change. Doug would probably believe he had encountered one malcontent. But if three or four staff members were to give messages of this type, and if the staff as a group ceased to "feign affection" and to be pleasant to Doug, then he might get the message that he had lost respect and must change his attitude to regain it.

Many people develop a sense of resignation in the face of less than optimal conditions in their families, schools, neighborhoods, agencies, and in their world in general. When it is suggested to them that they could take action to try to improve matters, they may reply, "It will not make any difference." They may subscribe to the idea "go along to get along." However, that is not the way in which the United States of America became a free nation. That is not the way in which women won the right to vote. That is not the way in which child labor laws were enacted. That is not the way in which any injustice was ever corrected. Refusing to feign affection for a person who misuses power or influence is but one in a sea of possibilities for improving our world, but it is one worth considering.

• • •

OFFERING ELEVEN

Neither be cynical about love,

for in the face of all aridity

and disenchantment

it is as perennial as the grass.

• • •

E hrmann's entreaty about love appears somewhat peculiar at first glance. He appears to be saying that love has negative qualities ("in the face of all aridity and disenchantment"), but that we should not be cynical about it because it comes around again ("It is as perennial as the grass"). That seems like telling someone who dislikes cold weather not to be cynical about winter since winter is a perennial season.

Be that as it may, love is a very important topic, and Ehrmann does have a point. Most people who have experienced love have in fact experienced the ways in which love can change from sweet to sour and can bring conflict, anger, and unhappiness. Yet even after such experiences, most people are repeatedly drawn to love. As Ehrmann states, it is perennial despite its tendency to lead to disenchantment.

Love is at the same time one of the most universally recognized but least understood concepts in our culture. Love is widely regarded as a powerful motivator of human endeavor and as an acceptable excuse for human frailty. But how often do we really inquire into the nature of love in general, or into the nature of one person's love for another in particular? The answer is, of course, rarely. We accept love, yet we misunderstand it as much as we recognize its importance and its influence.

The following is a list and brief description of what I consider to be six components of romantic love. Some of them are Greek concepts and I have included the Greek name for them. I hope that reading, considering, and talking about these six components will be helpful to couples who are considering making a commitment to one another, and to couples who are experiencing problems and trying to decide whether and how to stay together.

SIX Components of Romantic Love

ONE. For a love to develop and then to endure, partners must enjoy just being together and sharing interests and pastimes. The Greeks called this component of love "Agape," or friendship love. Romantic love usually involves affection and passion. But if affection and passion are to be durable, they must rest on firm foundations. One of those foundations is friendship. Even in the absence of affection, partners need to enjoy just being in one another's company and sharing thoughts, feelings, pastimes and experiences. The ability to share at least some interests, activities, and pastimes is an important part of an enduring romantic love. Although it is important to enjoy time spent together, balance is also important. It is not important, or even desirable, for persons to give up or de-emphasize their own interests that are not shared by their partner. But having some shared pastimes is crucial, so that partners will have many reasons to look forward to being together.

TWO. Another critical factor if love is to endure is appreciation for one another's skills, abilities, and personal characteristics. We can refer to this as respect. Although an over-idealized view of the partner's abilities is dangerous, it is still important for romantic lovers to appreciate, to a reasonable degree, one another's abilities. These abilities include good judgment and resourcefulness. If we are going to take the journey through life with a loved one at our side, we probably need to have confidence in that partner's ability to be a resource during that journey.

I will refer to affection and passion often, as they are so central, at least in the western world, to the concept of love. If affection and passion are strong enough, they can be so enthralling that they can influence a person's judgment. We can be so enthralled with affection and passion that we can make ourselves believe that they will be enough by themselves, and that we can overlook our partner's weaknesses in other areas. In relation to component number 2, we can convince ourselves that we can provide the resourcefulness that our partner may lack, and that we can be happy doing so as long as we have the affection and passion we desire. In my experience as a psychologist, I have seen persons who had become disenchanted with their partners' lack of resourcefulness, ultimately concluding that they had mistakenly ignored their partners' lack of those abilities.

THREE. This component is physical attraction, passion and mutual sensual pleasure, or what the Greeks called "Eros." This includes the play and pleasure aspect of love. Sometimes referred to as infatuation, this refers to the experience of thinking obsessively about the loved one, and the feeling of excitement at the thought of being with them. Early in a love relationship, this aspect, when powerful and delightful enough, can be solely responsible for the feeling of being in love. However, without the other components, this type of passion will turn out to have been more accurately defined as "infatuation" than as "love."

FOUR. The Greeks called this "pragma," or pragmatic love. This includes both a rational assessment of one another's assets and liabilities, and a sharing of goals, dreams and lifestyle considerations. Discussing this aspect of love can seem in a sense distasteful, but it is a reality. If you are going to buy a house, and you have $200,000 to spend, you will want to go into the housing market and get the best house $200,000 can buy. When we go out into "the relationship market," we do not go out with a dollar amount. Rather, we go out with our intelligence, education, appearance, sexual attractiveness, personality, family connections, material resources, sense of humor, and all our other attributes. Moreover, we want to find the most desirable partner that our attributes can attract. Again, it does not seem "nice" or in good taste to talk about it in these terms, but to ignore it is to ignore reality. Rather than ignore it, we serve ourselves better by analyzing which of a potential partner's attributes will make us happiest in the long run. For instance, while physical attractiveness is obvious and may be immediately pleasing, many personality factors may maintain love and affection better in the long term.

The sharing of goals, dreams and lifestyle considerations is the other part of pragmatic love. Do you want to make your education and profession a central feature of your life? Alternatively, would you prefer to leave work at work and emphasize your recreational, social or cultural lives? Do you want to establish a home and remain there? Or would you be happier relocating on occasion so as to expose yourself to new settings? On vacations and holidays do you want to get together with family, or do you prefer to travel? Agreement on at least a majority of lifestyle considerations is very important for a couple to remain happy with one another in the long run.

FIVE. Appreciation of, or even sharing of, values, philosophy, and view-of-the-world. This encompasses the deeper intellectual, or even spiritual, aspects of love. Although the demands of modern life tend to keep us focused on practical, strategic and mundane matters, there are those moments when many persons experience their lives on a deeper level. We may indulge in a spiritual life and reflect on the miracle of life and human existence. We may engage in religious thoughts and feelings, and wonder whether we are living up to the expectations of a deity. We may engage in idealistic, or Utopian fantasies, and imagine what an ideal school, community, nation or civilization would be like. Or, we may think deeply about what we value, and consider how we might best express those values in our society.

Even if the daily practical, strategic aspects of life predominate, there will be those opportunities for our values, goals, hopes, dreams, philosophy and view of the world to surface. For a passionate love to endure, it is very important that partners mutually respect one another's values, philosophy and worldview.

SIX. Good faith/good will/no "put downs"/genuine desire to enhance the happiness and self-esteem of the partner. Over the long haul, this is probably the most important component of romantic love if that love is truly to be passionate and enduring. Essentially, your partner's self-esteem needs to be among your highest priorities. As powerful as love can feel when it is working, love can be fragile. This is partly because we really do not understand the nature of love. We all live our lives from within our own skin and we experience life from our own perspective. The feeling of love we have for another person arises to a significant extent from the degree to which our loved one makes us feel good about ourselves. This idea may not be consistent with common myths about love, but understanding it will serve you better than the myths.

Partners need to learn to think about, and care about, one another's experience of daily life. And when one partner feels unappreciated or beaten up by the world, or feels less than fully competent, the other partner needs to be there to help their loved one feel better about himself or herself. Being there to understand one another's world, to comfort one another in times of distress, and to support one another's self esteem will in the final analysis be the most powerful factor in maintaining a romantic love.

Individuals often ask how many of these components describe deep friendship. If you subtract components three and four (physical attraction / mutual sensual pleasure, and pragmatic love), you probably have the components of a close and lasting friendship.

Individuals often ask how many components it takes for people to experience "falling in love." If component three (physical attraction / mutual sensual pleasure) and one other component, such as number one (mutual interests) are present; it is typical for persons to "fall in love." However, without the strong presence of other components, the "love" will probably turn out to have been infatuation, and an enduring, passionate love is unlikely.

Individuals often ask, "How can I know the difference between infatuation and love? Will love feel different?" Infatuation and love "feel" the same. The sense of desire and longing, the excitement, and the sense of being enraptured are the same. Recognizing the difference is a matter of thought and analysis, not a matter of feeling. Components two, four, five and six, which are important for a continuing romance, will be recognized by thinking, not by feeling.

With regard to love, individuals frequently ask, "Is it worth it?" Romantic love has the potential to bring us great joy as well as immense frustration and pain. Max Ehrmann exhorts us not to be cynical about love. I hope I have provided some information that will be helpful for couples who are in the process of developing a relationship. By considering and discussing the important components of love, perhaps partners can develop such a good understanding of one another that they will not have to experience disenchantment and cynicism.

• • •

OFFERING TWELVE

Take kindly the counsel

of the years,

gracefully surrendering the

things of youth.

● ● ●

The idea of taking kindly the counsel of the years requires no explanation. It simply means to learn from experience. However, the concept of "gracefully surrendering the things of youth" warrants a great deal of discussion. I believe there are many ways to "gracefully surrender," depending on your self-image, goals and lifestyle. Moreover, some of these ways are diametrically opposed to others. Let us look at three domains of life in which we can consider ways of surrendering the things of youth: style, health and fitness, and personal growth and development.

Style

Young persons in each succeeding generation tend to develop a style that, to a degree, defines them. This includes dress, hairstyle, grooming and speech patterns. Each generation takes on a style, or selection of styles, quite different from the generation that preceded it, but that may be strikingly similar to the style of the third or fourth generation before it. In the 1950s young people were clean shaven with crew cuts, and wore tapered slacks. In the 1960s the flower child generation wore bell-bottom pants and had long hair and beards. A few generations later, we saw shaven heads, and baggy "shorts" that went below the knees. For our purposes here, we do not have to be concerned about how and why our own generation developed its style. Our concern is to decide how and when to leave the youthful style of our generation behind us, and to develop our own personal, age-appropriate style.

I am sure you have seen grown adults who are still dressing and grooming themselves the way their peers did in their earlier years. There is no intent here to disparage that practice. However, you may have found yourself thinking it odd, and wondering when that person was going to "give it up" and be himself or herself. I would like to support the idea that gracefully surrendering the styles of youth does not entail abandoning one fad for another, but rather arriving at a style that suits us as an individual, and probably one that would be generally accepted as age-appropriate.

Health and fitness

This is a domain in which I believe there is a wide range of choices that may be considered graceful or not. For many persons, gracefully surrendering means less attention to strength and fitness. They may look back on their past and feel that they have accomplished what they wanted to in athletics and active recreation. They may desire rest and relaxation more than physical activity. They may pay less attention to healthy nutrition, feeling that they have earned a few more indulgences. Maintaining a fit or lean physique may no longer be a motivating force as physical attractiveness may be fading for them as a concern.

Other persons continue to strive for optimal health and fitness. They try to avoid food indulgences and strive to optimize the healthiness of their nutritional regimen. They keep up a fitness regimen, though it may well evolve as they mature. Brisk walking may take the place of running and jogging. Strength training may focus more on maintaining muscle tone than on building muscle bulk. They may give up timing and otherwise measuring their athletic endeavors, focusing more on their body's responses to the activity than on an external source of validation.

Again I ask, is Eros a "thing of youth"? Is acceptance of aging without fighting to stay healthy, fit and strong "graceful surrender," or is it more graceful to strive to maintain health and fitness? I would not presume to judge any individual's choice in this matter. However, I do believe that it is in our better interest to consider this matter carefully. With today's nutrition and healthcare, it is more possible for most persons to remain fit and strong into later years than would have been possible for prior generations. Physical fitness and recreational opportunities abound for mature adults. So, before deciding that strength and fitness are "things of youth," think about your priorities and your desires, and make a decision with which you are comfortable.

Growth and Development

Many persons, as they mature, "surrender the things of youth" in the sense that they cease to be invested in becoming more than they are. They feel that their life's accomplishments are behind them, and that they have no new worlds to conquer. And indeed, may persons have in fact had successful careers, provided for themselves materially, and brought up families. They may have accomplished all they had ever planned to, and they may be satisfied. For them, gracefully surrendering the things of youth may mean having fewer ambitions, and a reduced emphasis on new learning. It may mean a greater emphasis on accepting what they have become and accomplished, and on being content, and even complacent. For persons with children, this type of graceful surrender may entail paying more attention to and taking pride in the accomplishments of children and grandchildren, and less attention to personal pursuits or development.

On the other hand, many individuals would not consider the above-described attitude to be graceful. Many would consider it a relinquishing of the opportunity to continue to grow and develop. For many persons, devotion to new learning and new ambitions is a more graceful way of being.

In order to provide some perspective to these issues I will discuss the concepts of Eros and Thanatos. In Greek mythology, Eros is the son of Aphrodite and is the god of love. Sigmund Freud saw Eros as the drive toward sexuality and species preservation. I see it more broadly as the drive for life, love, growth, differentiation and development. Thanatos was the Greek god of death. Freud thought of Thanatos as a drive toward equilibrium, and he saw death as the final equilibrium. Thus in Freudian theory Thanatos is seen as the drive toward self-destruction and death. I see it in somewhat broader terms as the drive toward discouragement, disillusionment, depression, decay and eventual death. Freud identified these two concepts as drives that coexist, and are in conflict within the individual.

You may ask if there is there any reason to believe that these two drives really exist within us. Take a walk through the woods, and what do you see? You see sprouting, budding and growing things, and you see fallen trees and rotting logs. You see life and growth, and you see decay and death. Most people have heard of the concept of entropy. Entropy is a tendency, rather than a force per se, in nature. It is the tendency for energy to move from a state of greater organization to a state of lesser organization – to become less concentrated and more spread out. But it is clear that there is another tendency in the Universe besides entropy. Physicists and cosmologists have taught us that in the early Universe there was only hydrogen, helium, and a trace of lithium. Yet here we are, 13.7 billion years later, with about 100 elements in the periodic table, complex molecules, and life. Clearly, there is also a tendency in the Universe for things to become more complex, and this tendency is sometimes referred to as "emergence." Therefore, in nature, entropy and emergence are opposing tendencies. As we are a product of nature, it is reasonable to think that these two tendencies are present within us as well as around us. Thus, the drives of Eros and Thanatos sre consistent with scientific ideas and do make logical sense.

The idea of life and death instincts should not be confused with the Gestalt concept of contact and withdrawal. In Gestalt psychology, individuals are thought of as going through a cycle of contact, satisfaction and withdrawal. In fact, the cycle of contact and withdrawal is sometimes thought of as necessary to achieve clarity. Just as we have times of sleep and wakefulness . . . . . just as the tides come in and recede . . . . . and just as growing things bloom in spring and die back in winter . . . . . we have variations in our contact or immersion in experience. We can think of this as a natural rhythm of life. We exercise and then rest. We work hard and then relax. We engage in intense interpersonal experiences, and then take time to process. These experiences are not the same as expressions of life and death instincts – of Eros and Thanatos.

The question then is how may Eros and Thanatos manifest themselves. More than just the usual rhythm of life, Eros manifests itself as major efforts or tendencies toward life, enthusiasm, love, differentiation and growth. Examples:

- Maintaining a consistent exercise regimen,
- Learning about and practicing good nutritional habits,
- Taking academic courses and focusing your efforts on learning,
- Seeking new learning experiences,
- Working diligently at your occupation or profession,
- Leaving social events early enough to get sufficient sleep,
- Working toward greater understanding in relationships,
- Organizing your efforts to maintain order in your household and finances.
- Good decisions regarding risk and reward.
- Marshaling your resources to rebound when you feel down or depressed.
- Expressing optimistic views of your future.

Thanatos, on the other hand, manifests itself as either a lack of energy for life-enhancing pursuits, or behaving in health-reducing or dangerous ways. Examples:

- Failing to maintain an exercise regimen,
- Frequently indulging in unhealthy foods,
- Frequent and/or heavy intoxication,
- Apathetic attitude toward new learning,
- Complacency or laziness in your occupation or profession,
- Failing to get enough sleep,
- Allowing the household and/or finances to fall into disorder.
- Reckless driving,

- Poor decisions regarding risk and reward.
- Giving in and withdrawing when feeling down or depressed.
- Expressing pessimistic views about the future.

Is Eros a "thing of youth"? Is acceptance of aging without fighting to stay healthy, fit and ambitious "graceful surrender," or is it more graceful to strive to maintain health and fitness? Again, I would not presume to judge any individual's choice in this matter. But I do believe that it is in our better interest to consider this matter carefully. With today's nutrition and healthcare, it is possible for most persons to remain healthy and mentally sharp into later years than would have been possible in prior generations. Educational opportunities are available to mature adults through a variety of means. So, before deciding that growth and development are "things of youth," think about your priorities and your desires, and make a decision with which you are comfortable.

What can you do if you suspect that your proportion of Life Instinct versus Death Instinct is not as favorable as you would like? First, a comprehensive or detailed set of remedies is beyond the scope of this book. If you wish to maintain as much of the health and fitness of youth as you can, and are unsure of what methods to apply, you may wish to consult with a psychologist. With some assistance, you may be able to assess your attitudes, habits and strengths and come up with a plan to put your positive life instinct in the driver's seat.

Initiatives for Happiness

One method you may apply is to make a list of all possible life-enhancing interests and activities you can think of in five categories, as follows:

- Physical and recreational
- Enjoying the beauty of nature

- Your sense of curiosity and wonder about the natural world
- Culture: art, music, movies, television, history
- Social relationships.

If you make an effort to engage in pursuits in these five categories, you may experience increased happiness, increased zest for life, and a change in the relative strength of your life and death instincts. You may feel that your way of gracefully surrendering the things of youth does not preclude putting up a fight against certain aspects of maturing.

A Final Note

The concept of Eros versus Thanatos is one of many ways to conceptualize the complex organization of our thoughts, feelings, behavior and lifestyle. Think carefully about your health habits in such areas as exercise, nutrition, sleep, education, work, and relationships. If you feel your attitude and style regarding your own maturation are not as graceful as you would like, perhaps these concepts can serve as a wake-up call. Perhaps you can be more purposeful in developing a style of maturation that would better fit your personal definition of graceful maturation. But above all, in the gentle spirit of poet Ehrmann, be your own decision-maker, rather than believing that there is an external standard that you must meet.

• • •

OFFERING THIRTEEN

Nurture strength of spirit to shield you against sudden misfortune.

• • •

I will define strength of spirit as the ability to maintain some degree of equanimity, optimism and problem-solving skill in the face of adversity. The question: How can we nurture this ability? From the point of view of cognitive-behavioral psychology, the answer would be cognitive restructuring. This is a dollar and ninety-five-cent expression meaning, "training ourselves to think differently."

Approximately at the start of the Common Era, there was a school of thought in ancient Greece called the Stoic Philosophers. One of the first Stoic philosophers was Epictetus, who stated, "Humans are not influenced by events, but by the view we take of events." This is an extremely important concept. If we are influenced primarily by events, then we are left with no way to shield ourselves from sudden misfortune. However, if it is the view we take of events that has primary influence, then we can have more control over our reactions, since we can control, at least to some degree, how we view things.

Today, when we think of the word "stoic," we usually think of having or displaying no emotion at all. However, using the ideas that have evolved from the original stoic philosophy does not mean suppressing all emotion, but rather having the ability to reduce the strength of uncomfortable emotions. This is one of the roles of a branch of psychotherapy referred to as cognitive behavioral therapy.

Cognitive psychology in the modern era has approximately a fifty-year history. Some of the early proponents of the area were Aaron T. Beck (*Cognitive Therapy and the Emotional Disorders*) and Albert Ellis (*A new Guide to Rational Living, et cetera*). One basic concept of cognitive therapy is that thoughts precede emotion. We do not necessarily mean formal thoughts. We can have what Beck called "automatic thoughts," which are more like premises. If we wake up every morning with the expectation that everything in our day should go smoothly and without incident, we may call this a basic premise with which we are starting the day. If we leave for work and have a flat tire, we may respond with immediate anger or frustration. We did not have the time to formally think, "My life should and must go smoothly today, and this flat tire is an unbearable event because it is going against the way things should be." Nonetheless, those of us who are practitioners of cognitive behavioral therapy would still argue that the thought that "life should go smoothly" still precedes and causes the anger, even though it may have been a premise - an automatic thought.

We can refer to words such as "should, must, have to, and necessary" as imperatives. Imperatives in our thinking are at the root of most of our uncomfortable emotions, and interfere with our ability to nurture strength of spirit. In addition, they are just plain wrong. As Aaron Beck stated, "The anxious person is not merely emotionally disturbed; s/he is cognitively wrong." (Actually, he said "the neurotic," not "the anxious person," but that term is no longer in use). Albert Ellis compiled lists of what he considered the basic irrational beliefs of most human beings. He revised and shortened the list as his career evolved, and I will share just a few. One common irrational belief is, "I should be competent at all my endeavors." Pay attention. It is not irrational to say, "It sure would be great if I can be competent," or "There are many advantages of competence, so I'll strive for it." There is nothing at all irrational about those statements. The irrational statement is, "I should be competent."

There is no law in the Universe that states that any one of us should, must or ought to be competent. Competence is an advantage, and it is worth striving for. But it is not necessary; it is merely preferable. If you do not believe this, go out in the world and look around. Do you see a world full of competent people? If so, you do not live on the same planet on which I reside. In fact, I do not know one single person who is competent in all domains of life. However, you, I, and all the other people who are less than one hundred percent competent are still existing and going about our lives. Therefore, it is clearly not a requirement of the Universe that we be totally competent. Consider what it would be like to start your days with this premise: "Competence is an advantage, and I will strive to be as competent as I can. If I am less competent than I want to be in a given situation, I may be disappointed. But I am certain of three things. First, no one situation or event will define my entire life. Second, I am comfortable being less than perfect because that is the way every human being is. And third, being less than totally competent in any given situation is not a catastrophe." If that were the premise regarding competence that you awakened with each morning, you would indeed be in a position to shield yourself from sudden misfortune.

The same process would be true about another very common irrational belief: "I should and must be liked, admired and respected by all the persons whom I find significant." No matter how kind, intelligent, sociable and generous a person is, that person can never win the love, approval and admiration of everyone. And it is clearly not a requirement of nature that you, or anyone else, be universally admired. Therefore, we will have a much more comfortable life if we awaken with the premise, "Being liked and respected is an advantage, and I will strive to be as admirable as I can. If I am less admirable than I want to be in a given situation, I may be disappointed. But I am certain of three things. First, no one situation or event will define my entire life. Second, I am comfortable being less than perfectly admirable because that is the way every human being is. And third, being less than totally admirable in any given situation is not a catastrophe." If that were the premise regarding being liked, admired and respected with which you awakened each morning, you would indeed be in a position to shield yourself from sudden misfortune.

A third irrational belief that plagues most human beings is the idea that things should go well. The irrational belief may be described as follows: "People and events should turn out better than they do, and I have no choice but to be frustrated and unhappy when I am faced with life's grim realities." If we awaken every morning with the premise that our happiness depends on things going smoothly, we will have few, if any, happy days. We will have a much better chance to be contented and happy if we awaken with the premise, "Life is smoother and easier when things go well. I will hope for this, and will even put some effort into good planning and judgment. But if events do not turn out well, I will view this, properly, as an inconvenience. I will not see it as a catastrophe, and will certainly not see it as a sign that my life will be a never-ending series of difficulties."

When you experience an uncomfortable emotion, please do not try to squash that emotion. Let yourself experience it, while making sure that you are fully aware of your surroundings before expressing it. Later, when you have a chance to reflect on the experience, think about the precipitating event. Then recall your emotional response. Next, identify the irrational belief that could have been the actual cause of your emotion. Your irrational belief will be a variation on one of the fourteen irrational beliefs listed in Appendix B.

Your last task is the lynchpin of the operation. You will need to convince yourself of just how and why the irrational belief is, in fact, irrational. Use Appendix C, which contains a list of twenty-two responses to irrational beliefs. If you can train yourself to refute irrational beliefs effectively, and to awaken each morning with rational premises about life, you will have truly "nurtured strength of spirit to shield yourself against sudden misfortune."

• • •

OFFERING FOURTEEN

But do not distress yourself

with dark imaginings.

Many fears are born of fatigue

and loneliness.

. . .

This will be a continuation of my discussion on nurturing strength of spirit, as the concepts are related. In the previous section, we discussed nurturing strength of spirit by taking a rational and reasonable view of the world. We discussed not defining something as an unbearable catastrophe when it is, in fact, an inconvenience.

"Distressing yourself with dark imaginings" means, of course, focusing your attention on negative future outcomes. I will discuss three ways of coping with dark imaginings:

1. Preparation
2. Dealing with the catastrophic expectation
3. Dealing with loss and grief

First, however, we can realistically acknowledge that there are indeed possible negative future outcomes of situations. There is no one among us who could not become ill or injured tomorrow. Someone we love could become ill, injured, or could die. A natural disaster such as hurricane, typhoon, tornado, dust storm, tsunami, earthquake or coronal mass ejection could strike our region. Coping with dark imaginings does not mean pretending that misfortunes are impossible; it means realizing we will cope with them.

Preparation

Years ago when I was living in Georgia, my friend's daughter Daly was going to a college in north Georgia. Some high altitude areas in northern Georgia are subject to severe winter weather. Daly had to drive through a mountain pass at a significant elevation to get to school. Many vehicles went off the road in severe winter weather in that area. I told Daly to put four items in the trunk of her car: a sleeping bag, a bottle of water, a box of dried apricots and a "music roll" (that's family talk for a roll of toilet paper). That way, if she were unlucky and went off the road, she would be warm, fed, watered, and could take care of her hygiene. Her response was an impatient, "I don't want to worry about that!" I replied, "I don't want you to worry, either. And if you will take the preparations I have suggested, there will be little to worry about."

For some reason, Daly was equating preparation with worry, and she is not alone. Many people fail to prepare for foreseeable problems. There are many potential problems for which there is no way to prepare. However, when preparation is an attainable proposition, taking the steps to prepare may make it easier for us to let go of those particular "dark imaginings."

Dealing with the Catastrophic Expectation

You have undoubtedly heard someone say, "I like to expect the worst and hope for the best." This is their way of saying that they want to have prepared themselves for the catastrophic expectation.

Individuals will often have a growing sense of anxiety and apprehension about some upcoming appointment, deadline or event. Frequently, they cannot identify the cause of their apprehension. When fears are formless and nameless, they can have an impact on us far greater than if we were able to give them a shape and a name. I often use the following analogy:

> It seems that the cause of your fears is hidden from you. Something of which you are unaware is repelling you. It is as though you were seeking something hidden beneath some slimy, mucky mud. You are afraid to go after it, because you fear it will be slimy and horrible. Finally, you dig into the mud and pull up some slimy, mucky roots. However, after you brush off the mud, in the sunshine and the dry air the roots dry up and flake away. When you are fearful of something unknown, it can seem horrible, like your fear of the roots under the mud. But when you confront your fears and bring them out into the open, they often lose their power, just as the slimy roots dried up and flaked away in the sun and dry air.

When helping a client to deal with a catastrophic expectation, a therapist will often ask, "What is the worst thing that can happen?" The worst thing may indeed be a very painful, disruptive, or tragic event. However, when brought to light and discussed, it will exert less power over you than it does when it is left unattended. One thing that gives "dark imaginings" their power is the idea that they represent a horrendous, emotionally non-survivable event. We think we will be unable to survive the experience – "unable to stand it." How many times in your life have you ever said, or thought, the words, "I can't stand it." Most individuals admit that they have either said or thought those words hundreds, or even thousands, of times. Moreover, how many times were you right? The answer: zero. You "stood it" every single time. However, when you indoctrinate yourself with the idea that you "cannot stand it," you are truly giving a great deal of power to a "dark imagining."

Coping with loss and grief

Grief is the emotional and physical reaction to any loss of significance. We usually associate grieving with the loss of a loved one through death. However, there are other types of losses that may also pre-cipitate a grief reaction:

*** loss of social contact (e.g. separation, divorce, a friend moving far away)
*** retirement (loss of youth, career, ambitions, plans, dreams)
*** disability (loss of full functional ability)
*** children growing up and leaving home (loss of nurtur-ing role)

We may even have a mild, fleeting grief reaction to trading in an old car or losing a watch we have been wearing for many years. Obviously, some losses have far more impact than others do. But all losses of significance tend to cause an emotional reac-tion, and recognizing this can be very helpful for us. Although we recognize that grief is a reaction to any loss of significance, our discussion will relate mostly to bereavement, the loss of a loved one through death.

In our American culture, we try to deny the reality of death. Consider the use of the phrase "If anything ever happens to me" instead of the more direct phrase "If I die." Consider also the last line of our stories: "And they lived happily ever after." No one lives happily ever after. Try this: "They lived long, healthy, happy lives and finally died at peace and with dignity." It may sound peculiar at first, but it is honest, accurate and, in my opinion, far more healthy. Consider also how far we lagged behind other countries such as England in developing a hospice movement. In hospice care, persons dying, as well as their families, can go through the dying process with more comfort, more honesty, less deception, and fewer unnecessary and invasive procedures performed on a person who needs comfort and dignity, not cure.

> **There is but one freedom - to come
> to terms with death - after which,
> everything is possible.**
> **--Albert Camus**

Individuals often wonder if it is good to cry after someone near them dies. It is more than just good. It is very important. A grief reaction seems to be almost a physiological necessity. Trying to suppress a normal grief reaction usually brings about emotional and medical problems later on. We will experience a great deal in a normal grief reaction.

- A sense of emotional pain, building like a wave and then subsiding
- A pronounced need to sigh
- Fatigue
- Loss of appetite. Food may taste like straw. Throat may feel constricted
- A tendency to think over and over about the last contact with the deceased
- A preoccupation with what the last moments of life were like for the deceased
- Anger (at fate, nature, the deity, or even anger at the deceased)
- Feeling abandoned (by the deceased)

- Loss of pleasure and interest
- Denial of the reality of the death

These symptoms can probably not be avoided. You may, however, delay them. For instance, there is often a "designated caretaker" in a family after a death. This person may make funeral arrangements, inform the newspaper, arrange family gatherings, handle legal and financial matters, and be sure everyone else is okay. This person may feel that s/he has no time to cry and grieve, and may be viewed as "strong." However, after all the family gatherings are concluded and everyone else has had opportunity to cry and grieve, the "strong" caretaker may be left feeling empty, and will almost undoubtedly end up with a delayed or "atypical" grief reaction.

Delayed or "atypical" grief reactions include all the symptoms typical of normal grieving, with a few unfortunate extras:

- A pervasive feeling of impending doom
- Taking on some of the symptoms of the deceased's final illness (this is especially true in an "anniversary reaction")
- Inability to concentrate due to preoccupation with the image of the deceased
- Anger, irritability
- Unnatural cheerfulness, frenetic energy, grandiose plans
- Wooden facial expression
- Loss of emotion
- Depression

**The more absolute death seems
The more authentic life becomes.
-- John Fowles**

People often question what they should do about things that remind them of their deceased loved ones, such as their belongings, or pictures of them. The short answer is: Do not go to extremes. Do not leave their clothing in the closet for the next year. Do not give away, donate, or sell all their prized possessions. Keep a few mementos. Keep that favorite bathrobe or sweatshirt but do not keep an overwhelming amount. Keep a favorite tool but not the entire set. Keep some of their pictures in the house, but do not leave their bedroom, study or office intact as a kind of shrine. Practice moderation.

Persons who are bereft often ask if it is healthy to make a practice of visiting the grave. This is a matter of personal preference. Many persons can invoke an image of the deceased whenever and wherever they are, can carry on an imagined conversation with the deceased at any time, and therefore have no real need to visit a grave. Other individuals may find it difficult to bring back their sense of the deceased and to work through their feelings. Visiting the grave can be very helpful for these persons.

Bereft individuals sometimes find themselves carrying on a conversation with a deceased person, and they wonder if this is unhealthy. It is not unhealthy if you know that the deceased is not actually physically present with you. Your emotions are of paramount importance. By "talking to the deceased" you may help yourself to truly feel and to work through emotions that could otherwise remain blocked and stuck within you. Blocked emotions can cause you emotional difficulties.

It is common for bereft persons to feel anger at the deceased. They are uncomfortable with that emotion, fearing that it is unfair and inappropriate. Your feelings are never, in and of themselves, unfair or inappropriate. You always have a right to your feelings. Anger toward the deceased is often part of what we call "unfinished business." Although issues can no longer be actually negotiated with the deceased, your feelings can nonetheless be worked through, and your "unfinished business" can to at least some extent be emotionally resolved.

A few last points:

- The deceased was once a part of your physical world and will continue to be part of your emotional world.
- Do not avoid the subject of a deceased person – your loved one or someone else's. Talk about them. Tell stories about them. Laugh about them. Go from tears to laughter and back to tears again. All this is appropriate and healthy. Avoiding the subject is unhealthy.
- Holidays and the deceased's birthday will be difficult for a year, or even two. Do not even try to avoid the subject and to avoid tears. It will be an exhausting effort that will stifle everyone's ability to be natural. Make the statement that "It sure is sad that xxxx isn't with us," cry, and then get on with the day. You will have more emotional flexibility.
- The "wave of emotional pain" that accompanies grieving will not overwhelm you, though at first it may feel that it will. The feelings will subside. Let them pass through you.

We have considered three ways of trying not to distress ourselves with dark imaginings: preparation, dealing with the catastrophic expectation, and dealing with loss and grief. These are but three of the myriad ways the topic of "dark imaginings" could have been explored. I hope that you will be better equipped to avoid distressing yourself with dark imaginings, having read and considered the ideas that have been presented.

• • •

OFFERING FIFTEEN

Beyond a wholesome discipline, be gentle with yourself.

• • •

Ehrmann is obviously talking about self-discipline. When I am asked what it is that I am trying to help therapy patients to attain, I sometimes answer, "Awareness, joy, productivity, meaning and relatedness." Tucked right in the middle of those five goals is "productivity," which implies a degree of self-discipline. Self-discipline is also a wonderful trait when we are striving to attain things other than productivity, such as health, physical prowess, improved relationships, or increased knowledge. The questions, then, are, "How much self-discipline is wholesome?" and "At what point is self-discipline more like self-oppression?"

There are two sources of possible answers to those questions: within and without. That is, you may look inside yourself and be the judge of what entails wholesome discipline. Or, you can look to some outside source for guidance. In his book **When I Say "No" I Feel Guilty**, Manuel Smith suggests a bill of assertive rights. The first assertive right is:

> You have the right to be the judge of your
> thoughts, feelings and behavior, and to
> take the responsibility for their initiation
> and their consequences for yourself.

As a starting point, think of yourself as having the right to judge how much self-discipline is wholesome. But, are there circumstances in which it is appropriate to look outside yourself for criteria as to an acceptable level of self-discipline? Unless you live in total isolation, the answer is yes. If you are married or otherwise attached, and share a common destiny with another, your partner has a right to expect some level of self-discipline from you. If you have a child, there is a reasonable expectation that you attain sufficient self-discipline to look after your child's safety, education, medical needs, and need for love and security.

For persons living conventional lives in our industrialized society, there are many demands on your self-discipline. Teachers or professors will demand discipline in study. Supervisors will demand discipline at task performance. Municipalities and the IRS will demand discipline at paying taxes. Local authorities will demand discipline at adherence to codes and ordinances. The list goes on. Then there are our expectations of ourselves for performance in athletics and fitness, social skill, academic and professional attainment, financial success, and ethical responsibility. And that list goes on. How can you determine when you have attained a wholesome degree of self-discipline?

You may note the similarity of this issue with that in our discussion of "gracefully surrendering the things of youth." We were discussing the degree to which it is graceful to continue to strive for new health, fitness, learning, growth and development. During that prior discussion, I introduced the Gestalt concept of contact and withdrawal. That is a relevant concept to the idea of a wholesome discipline. A wholesome discipline is one that allows for some degree of withdrawal after a period of contact. That is, it allows for a period of rest, relaxation, recreation, or some form of self-renewal after a period of work and productivity.

There is no certain answer to this question, but I will suggest an approach to the issue. First, be aware of how you feel about your level of self-discipline. Secondly, set some objective standards by which to help assess your self-discipline. Then, strive for a balance between the two – between your feelings and your objective standards. From your own individual experience, you may be aware of whether your feelings or your objective standards have the deciding vote. Above all, keep in mind the poet Ehrmann's entreaty: "Be gentle with yourself."

• • •

OFFERING SIXTEEN

You are a child of the Universe,

No less than the trees

and the stars.

You have a right to be here.

• • •

We are children of the Universe in a very literal sense. Our knowledge of the Universe has grown by enormous leaps and bounds since Galileo first aimed his telescope at the Moon and saw that, rather than a perfect sphere, the Moon has craters and mountains. We now have well-established theories about the origin and evolution of the Universe. For our purposes here, the important ideas have to do with the origin of the elements, and this is a particularly well supported part of science. In the early Universe, the only elements that existed were hydrogen, helium, and a trace of lithium. However, we are composed of a variety of elements, including carbon, oxygen, sodium, chlorine, calcium, magnesium, potassium, phosphorous, manganese, iron, zinc, selenium, and iodine.

Where do these elements come from, if they were not present in the early Universe? The answer concerns the nature of stars. You can call a star a gravitationally bound fusion reactor. Right now, as you read these words, our star – the Sun – is converting fifty-five million tons of hydrogen into fifty million tons of an isotope of helium every second. Five million tons of matter exits the Universe, converted into energy (specifically, gamma rays), at a rate described by Albert Einstein's famous equation e = mc-squared. When our Sun runs out of available hydrogen in its core (perhaps six or more billion years from today), it will begin to fuse helium into carbon. Our star is a medium mass star. It will not fuse elements heavier than carbon. However, very massive stars go through a series of oscillations, and every time they run out of one type of nuclear fuel, they begin fusing the next heavier element. Especially massive stars continue this process until they have fused iron. At this point, they will become a type II supernova, exploding with enough heat and pressure to fuse all the heavy elements right up to uranium. Those elements are scattered through interstellar space. When interstellar clouds of gas and dust that contain heavy elements become gravitationally unstable and fall in on themselves, they form new stars, with planetary systems. These new stars - known as second or third generation stars - and their planets contain heavy elements. Our Sun, the Earth and the other planets of our Solar System obviously contain heavy elements, and that has made life possible. The very elements that comprise our bodies were "cooked up" in former generations of stars.

Therefore, when Max Ehrmann tells you that you are a child of the Universe, he is correct literally as well as figuratively. I hope that when you consider these ideas, you will realize that, in a sense, the Universe has gone to a great deal of trouble to make our existence possible. Whether or not you believe this process was directed by a conscious being, it is a wonderful and miraculous process. Knowing about it can give us a sense of wonder and gratitude about life – our own life . . . our neighbor's life . . . anyone's life.

• • •

And, whether or not it is clear

to you

No doubt the Universe is unfolding

as it should.

· · ·

This is a very challenging concept to discuss, given the vast-ly different beliefs, philosophies and feelings people have about life. Recall that in Offering Thirteen we addressed the con-cept of "imperatives" - of the meaning and uses of words such as "should, must, have to and necessary." Rather than recapitulate what we addressed in that offering, I will take a different tack. I believe a good way to address this issue is to make it more about **us** than about the Universe.

It is sometimes said that philosophers ask five questions:

1. Is it true?
2. Is it just?

3. Is it beautiful?
4. Is it good?
5. Is it real?

When we state that there is a way the Universe "should unfold," we are probably stating that we want the world to unfold in a way that is just, beautiful and good. It does not take a thorough and detailed study of human history and current events to convince us that the unfolding of events is not always just, beautiful and good. If we have a requirement in our minds that the Universe **should** unfold in a way that is just, beautiful and good, we are setting ourselves up for major disappointment and disillusionment. If we take away our requirement that the Universe be just, beautiful and good, we lessen our sense of injustice and dissatisfaction.

When we assert that there is a way in which the world should behave, we are issuing a directive to a Universe that does not obey our commands. This puts us under what can be a great sense of strain. I believe that Ehrmann's entreaty is not that we should convince ourselves that everything in the world is just, beautiful and good, but that we should accept that the Universe will unfold as it will despite our desires or our demands. I believe he is essentially saying, "No doubt you can learn to accept the unfolding of the Universe without protest."

• • •

OFFERING EIGHTEEN

Therefore be at peace

with your God

Whatever you conceive

him to be.

. . .

This book is intended to be an application of Ehrmann's *Desiderata* to psychological well-being. It is not intended to be a theological treatise. As Ehrmann indicates by his words "whatever you conceive him to be," he is aware of the many different conceptions of god.

The words, "Be at peace with your god, whatever you conceive him to be," seems to be a continuation of the previous lines about the Universe unfolding as it should. Sadly, among the seven billion-plus human beings on the Earth, there are billions whose situations in life, whether chronic or temporary, would make it very challenging for them to be at peace with their god. From a psychological perspective, it would be potentially destructive to insist that an individual be at peace with his or her god if they are living under painful circumstances.

Consider some of the circumstances under which people are living:

- Volcanoes, earthquakes or tsunamis may have laid waste to their homes and communities.
- Wars, whether political/military or drug-related, have resulted in deaths of loved ones.
- Parents have seen their children die of violence or disease.
- Governments or other "authorities" have kidnapped their loved ones or taken their homes.
- People are suffering pain and misery without medical or psychological aid.
- People are living in abject poverty, with little food and no clean water.

Certainly, some people do have a way of viewing their lives and the world that will allow them to be at peace with their god despite extreme deprivation. However, it would be presumptuous and insensitive to suggest it to them as their duty. Perhaps we have to assume that Ehrmann, who was educated in the American northeast and lived in the American Heartland, was speaking to those of us who are fortunate enough not to be living under circumstances of extreme pain, poverty, injustice, or deprivation. Surely, for those of us in fortunate circumstances, it is easier to be at peace with our god.

Many people conceive of a god who remains aware of the circumstances of every being, and who can be petitioned with prayer. There are many, termed "deists," who believe that a supreme being gave the world its start, and then backed off to let the world evolve on its own. Alternatively, there are many who have a sense that the Universe did in fact go to great lengths to allow us our existence. They may feel a sense of gratitude about existence, but may not see human qualities in the forces in the Universe that allowed our existence.

Being at peace with your god will depend to some degree on "whatever you conceive him to be," and to some degree on the circumstances in which you find yourself.

Albert Einstein, known as a deeply spiritual man, wrote the following:

> I cannot believe in a god who rewards or punishes his creatures, or who has a will of the kind we experience in ourselves. I am satisfied with the mystery of the eternity of life, and with a glimpse of the marvelous structure of the existing world, together with the continued striving to comprehend a portion, be it ever so tiny, of the Reason that manifests itself in nature.

Einstein clearly had a profound desire to understand the Universe. In his view, a "glimpse of the marvelous structure of the existing world," along with striving to comprehend it, was satisfying. Since he stated he was satisfied with this, we can say that to at least some degree he was at peace with his god. May you be as fortunate.

• • •

OFFERING NINETEEN

And whatever your labors

and aspirations

In the noisy confusion of life,

Keep peace in your soul.

With all its sham, drudgery and

broken dreams,

It is still a beautiful world.

Be cheerful. Strive to be happy.

. . .

As in the previous offering, if we accept the idea that it is a beautiful world, we are probably among those citizens of the world who are fortunate enough not to live in an area recently ravaged by natural disaster or acts of war. And we will assume we are fortunate enough not to live in intractable pain, abject poverty, or with extreme injustice or deprivation. Assuming that we are among the fortunate, we can more easily consider the beauty of the world. Beauty is not, of course, an innate feature of the world. It is a concept that we impose on the world by our perceptions. We can choose to perceive beauty where we wish. Moreover, we can choose to experience beauty through all our senses as well as through our knowledge.

We may choose to **see** beauty in countless places including the following:

- A sunset or sunrise
- A starlit sky
- Sunlight sparkling off the surface of a lake, pond or ocean
- Rolling, green fields
- Mountain tops
- A bird in flight
- A whale or dolphin surfacing in the ocean
- A brightly colored butterfly.

We may choose to **hear** beauty in countless places including:

- Birdsong
- The whispery, feathery sound of spring leaves in a breeze
- The crisp rustling of autumn leaves in a breeze
- The sound of surf rolling in on an ocean beach
- The sound of crickets on a summer evening
- The sound of a stream or brook

We may **feel** beauty:

- A warm, gentle summer breeze against our face and through our hair

- The crisp air on our face on an autumn day
- The soft texture of grass under our feet
- The rush of water around our body as we dive into water

We may **smell or taste** beauty:

- The fragrance of flowers
- Fresh, salty sea air
- The explosive flavor of a strawberry
- Chocolate

We may **know** beauty through our intellect. We may enjoy knowledge about:

- the evolution of the Universe
- the origin of the elements
- the formation of the Earth
- the geologic periods of Earth's history
- the variety of species in the plant and animal kingdoms
- the intricacies of the human genome

I chose to list natural sources of beauty, as opposed to those created by human hands, but human creations can also be part of what we experience as beauty in the world. Moreover, the beauty of human kindness and generosity is certainly worthy of our appreciation. As the poet Ehrmann notes, we do experience labors and aspirations, and this is in the context of the "noisy confusion of life." Whatever are the sources of your personal experiences of beauty, poet Ehrmann is entreating you to remember them as a way to "keep peace in your soul."

Ehrmann's final exhortation is "Be cheerful. Strive to be happy." (If you should find a number of versions of *Desiderata*, you will find that some of them state, "Be careful. Strive to be happy." I have found "Be cheerful" more often, and it seems to be a more appropriate fit. Thus, I have written, "Be cheerful"). The expression "strive to be happy" is worthy of note, as there are a number of ways in which we may enhance our strivings for happiness. In Appendix A – Fifteen Principles for Happiness – principle number nine is as follows:

> Principle for Happiness NINE: If we want to drink the wine of life with any gusto, it probably takes some hard work and self-discipline. No one has ever achieved optimal human happiness by just sitting around trying to passively or uncommittedly enjoy him or herself.

There are many ways in which we can exercise the self-discipline of striving to be happy. You have already been introduced to the ideas of brainstorming initiatives for happiness, and also to Fifteen Principles for Happiness. A final technique in the happiness repertoire is described in Appendix D: Daily Boosts for Happiness. This method involves boosting our happiness in six ways. The idea is to enjoy each of the following:

- A moment to enjoy the beauty of nature
- A moment of relaxation
- A moment to enjoy music
- A moment to enjoy humor
- A moment of bliss (think about one of the Fifteen Principles for Happiness)
- Performing a random act of kindness

The six daily boosts, described in more detail in Appendix D, can be exercised a number of times per day. Each time, you will find you have given your mood a boost, and you will have honored poet Ehrmann's entreaty, "Strive to be happy."

You may remember Roy. In Offering Seven we were discussing the concept of "process versus product." We described Roy's method for making the most of the summer months. Roy also has a habit of running through the six daily boosts for happiness. He described one such episode as follows:

> I was driving to work, and I found myself feeling emotionally a bit on the low side. I began to look at the trees and the clouds. I saw a stand of trees that had a particularly pleasing appearance, and I really took in that beauty. Then I took a slow, deep breath. As I exhaled, I thought "serene." Then I imagined tension draining away, the way water might drain through a pipe, leaving me with a sense of stillness, like a pond without a ripple. I have very good memory of sounds, so I then "played" some of Beethoven's Pastoral Symphony for myself in my head, until I felt a sense of the beauty of that music. Next, I recalled one of my favorite *Peanuts* cartoons, and I laughed aloud. Then I thought about Principle for Happiness Number four, and I reminded myself of how lucky I am not to live in a war zone or other truly devastating situation. Finally, I saw a person in a car, trying to pull out of a driveway into the traffic, and I slowed down and waved him ahead. Having made those six quick boosts, I found myself feeling cheerful and happy, whereas I had been a little down five minutes earlier.

The Six Daily Boosts for Happiness can be used a number of times during the course of a day. Every time you do so, you are likely to have given your mood an upward boost. Whether you believe we are here by Divine Providence or as an inevitable result of the laws of nature, we are here. Moreover, as long as we are here, we may as well make the most of the opportunity. Making the most of it may mean seeking awareness, joy, productivity, meaning and relatedness. There is no reason to believe that joy and happiness are not among our legitimate pursuits. Poet Ehrmann speaks to us from the last century, and encourages us to be happy. I hope that by writing this book I have enhanced the ways in which Max Ehrmann's gentleness of spirit continues into the present. I hope I have given you ideas of how to take Ehrmann's encouraging words and to put them into practice in a meaningful and effective way to increase your happiness.

• • •

Appendix A

15 Principles for Happiness

© by Michael R. Slavit, Ph.D., 1993

<u>Introduction</u>

H ave you ever had the experience of witnessing something that made you feel very lucky? (A typical example cited by many people is feeling grateful and happy to have two sound legs after seeing someone in a wheel chair). Almost everyone has these experiences, and everyone reports the same occurrence, that the feelings of luck, gratitude and happiness soon fade away.

There are many experiences that give us a moment of perspective, in which our own condition in life seems good, resulting in a feeling of increased happiness. The idea of Fifteen Principles for Happiness is to provide you with a ready-made set of perspectives to help you to re-create those moments of increased happiness.

Please read the fifteen principles described below, and then the suggestions at the end.

ONE.   It's all a bonus. If you have ever had a narrow escape from death, then you know that, in a sense, you are fortunate just to be alive. Even if you are having a generally unsuccessful day, there may be a few moments of pleasure or contentment. Those moments are a bonus. Therefore, regardless of what happens in your life today, tell yourself that every moment of pleasure or contentment is a bonus. You have much more than you would have had if you were no longer alive.

TWO.   It's not **my** world; it's **the** world. When you feel unhappy or frustrated about the state of things in the world around you, protect yourself from any sense of personal failure. Don't take it personally that it's not a better world. It is, after all, not your world, but just the world.

THREE.   Humor. Have you ever said or thought the following: "Someday I'll look back on this and laugh"? Why wait? Laugh now, even if the only humor you can see in the situation is the humor of the absurd.

FOUR. Do you remember January of 1991? It was the start of Operation Desert Storm - the Persian Gulf War. Have you wondered what it would have felt like to have lived in occupied Kuwait during the Persian Gulf War? We probably would have felt absolute terror every day. Regardless of what you have to face today, it is probably not too bad when put into that perspective.

FIVE. Picture a group of hikers out for a walk. A bee hive is disturbed and a dozen bees come swarming out and sting . . . one hiker. Why that one?!? Answer: random. We all get some bad luck, and it is best not to take it personally when you get yours . . . best not to feel as though life, fate or nature ganged up on you personally.

SIX. Imagine a hospital patient, on his deathbed, dying of stress related disease. He looks up before dying and sees, on his bedside table, a glass of water - half full. Before dying he smiles to himself and says, "Here I am, dying of stress related disease, because I spent my entire life seeing that glass as half empty instead of half full." It is best to accept the fact that the glass will always be half empty - that there will always be some imperfections in your life. But there are always some aspects of your life which can make you feel happier - if you will let yourself enjoy them.

SEVEN. If there is such a thing as heaven on Earth, it comes when we are fully aware that life is a process and not a product. Your life is not a resume ... not a portfolio ... not a house under construction. The expression "my life is ruined" is possible only when we feel life is a product instead of what it is in reality - a succession of moments for us to experience.

EIGHT. Imagine a big wrought iron gate, or fence. Inside the fence is a park in which people are very happy, playing, sing-ing, and relaxing. A person is trying to climb over the gate and into the park, but cannot make it because s/he is carrying excess baggage. The baggage consists of the demands and expecta-tions of the (dead) past and the (imagined) future. We can make it into the happy park as long as we can prevent our conscious-ness from being dominated by the demands and expectations of the dead past and the imagined future.

NINE. If we want to drink the wine of life with any gusto, it probably takes some hard work and self-discipline. No one has ever achieved optimal human happiness by just sitting around trying to passively or uncommittedly enjoy themselves.

TEN. Imagine a den of lions eating their kill. The operant word here is "kill," or death. We will all die. Between now and then we will have many feelings, and we have a right to all of them, no matter what they are. However, if we are indulging often in certain negative feelings such as feeling put down, put upon, cheated, angry, hateful, et cetera, we may want to ask ourselves how much of our precious time we want to devote to those feelings.

ELEVEN. Imagine a quarterback with his team pushed all the way back to his own 5 yard line. He desperately wants to score a touchdown, so he keeps throwing long passes. The defense, sensing what is happening, defends easily, and the quarterback fails. If he had been content to throw short passes, he might have picked up 6, 8, or 10 yards every play. The point: take what the defense gives you. Be satisfied with small steps of progress toward your ultimate goals and desires if, as is usually the case, you cannot achieve them all at once.

TWELVE. Imagine a trophy shelf with all the trophies signifying a person's accomplishments. But they are all jumbled in together and look like a mess. On the wall nearby is a simple, elegant plaque which states that this person has reasonable values ... and lives by them. In the final analysis we are probably happiest if we know who we are - know what we value - and live accordingly.

THIRTEEN. Imagine a person with a sprained wrist. He wanted to do carpentry that day, but cannot. First he bandages the wrist, but then immediately turns his attention to other activities that he can enjoy without strenuous use of his wrist. The point: do not ignore the parts of your life that are going poorly. Take at least one step toward improving things. Then consider turning your attention to matters that are going well and that can bring you happiness now.

FOURTEEN. Imagine two lovers on a park bench. But they are not busy courting; they are staring at some people doing Tai Chi in the park. Tai Chi, an eastern martial art form, involves slow, elegant motions. The point: We are probably more efficient and happier when we do things in a moderately-paced, well-considered, elegant way than when we do things in a rushed, hectic, helter-skelter way.

FIFTEEN. Imagine a weight lifter, looking in the mirror and comparing himself to other weight lifters. The idea here has to do with comparisons. When we compare ourselves to others, we get one of two results. Either we judge ourselves superior and feel vain or we judge ourselves inferior and feel deprived. Neither feeling will make us happy. Some comparisons are inevitable, but it will be in our better interest to limit them if we can.

Suggestions

1. Review all fifteen principles twice a day for two days.

2. After the second day, select a shorter list of between five to eight of the principles that seem most meaningful for you.

3. Continue to review your selected list twice a day. Give the ideas a chance to sink in to the point that you can feel them intuitively or "in your gut." It is not enough to just repeat the words (e.g. "It's all a bonus ..... yeah, it's a bonus"). Stay with the thoughts until you can really feel them. Just one of these principles can lift your spirits at any given time. Principle #9 emphasizes that happiness takes some hard work and self-discipline. Work conscientiously at this exercise and ... feel happier.

Appendix B
Typical Irrational Beliefs

Michael R. Slavit, Ph.D, ABPP.
Board Certified in Cognitive and Behavioral Psychology

Thoughts precede emotions. Oftentimes the thoughts with which we evaluate situations are more in the nature of premises than formal thoughts. There are certain irrational thoughts or premises that most of us have and that can result in considerable emotional distress. Only by finding and actively, tirelessly refuting these irrational thoughts can we learn to avoid unnecessary emotional distress. The following are fourteen typical irrational, destructive thoughts. It will help you to find the thoughts that you do believe deep down inside. Then, you can help yourself considerably by starting a vigorous campaign to challenge and eliminate irrational thoughts.

1. Since competence is a desirable trait, it is therefore necessary that I be competent in every situation. If I am incompetent in any one instance, it is positive proof that I am not a desirable and worthwhile person.

2. It is nice to be liked, admired and respected. Therefore I must have approval from all persons I think are significant.

3. Personal dignity absolutely depends on always appearing to be in control. To be in any way incapacitated or dependent while observed by others would surely make it impossible for those others to ever again view me as a dignified person. My life as a person of dignity would be forever destroyed by any observed loss of control.

4. If I am seriously frustrated, treated unfairly or rejected, I cannot merely view it as unfortunate and painful. I must view it as horrible and catastrophic.

5. It is an absolute necessity that fairness and justice prevail in all situations. To be faced with an uncorrectable wrong is unspeakably frustrating and miserable.

6. People and events should turn out better than they do. If I am faced with something that does not turn out as well as I want it to, then I have no choice but to feel miserable.

7. Convenience and comfort are preferable to inconvenience and discomfort. If I am subjected to inconvenience or discomfort, then things are not as they should be and I have to feel miserable about it.

8. If I am awaiting some future decision, test, diagnosis, or any other potentially stressful event, I have to stay on my guard. This means that I cannot distract myself with anything pleasurable or interesting. I must preoccupy myself with what is to come and I must make myself anxious about it.

9. My past remains all-important. If something once strongly influenced my life, it must go on controlling my feelings and behavior today. There can be no remedy.

10. It is impossible to feel physical pain without feeling emotional misery.

11. There is a right way and a wrong way to live. If I do not do what is right, then I must feel a pervasive and inescapable sense of wrongness.

12. Once I establish a workable routine, that routine must be maintained.

13. My role in this world is indispensable. For me to be unable to fulfill my role would bring about horrible, unspeakable consequences.

14. I always know in advance when a situation is so bad that nothing can make it better.

Appendix C

Ways to Refute Irrational Beliefs

Almost all of us learned early in life to believe things that are not true. We can call these thoughts "irrational beliefs." They are irrational for a number of reasons, including

1. There is no evidence to support them;
2. They assume we can predict the future;
3. They assume that either we or the world can be perfect; and
4. They are rigid and absolutistic, and ignore the way the world really is.

When we awaken each day we have a set of beliefs about life. In this book, we have discussed common irrational thoughts. When things happen, right away we judge things based on these beliefs. For that reason Dr. Aaron T. Beck called them "automatic thoughts." Because they are quick and automatic, it is very difficult to change them "on the spur of the moment" when an event occurs. Our best strategy is to change them ahead of time, by convincing ourselves of the truth of some rational, coping thoughts.

Following are 22 rational, coping thoughts that can defeat irrational, automatic thoughts. First, review this list twice/

day for two days. Really look closely at these ideas. After two days, please make a selection of the rational, coping ideas that are most powerful for you. Choose the ideas that really help you to see how false irrational thoughts are, and that help you see the world in a different light. Choose between FIVE and EIGHT of the coping thoughts that help you the most. You may want to create a memory device that will help you bring these ideas quickly to mind. In this way, you will turn your favorite coping thoughts into a powerful working philosophy, rather than just leaving them as "something you once read."

1. There are many things in life that are advantageous and preferable. Assuming that life itself is necessary, necessities are breathing, eating, drinking, sleeping and eliminating. Everything else, no matter how preferable, is not necessary.

2. I have often had reactions that basically meant, "This should not be this way." The truth: if the world required things to be different, they would be different. There is no reason things should or must be different from the way they are.

3. It is preferable for me to be liked and admired. But not everyone will like, admire or respect me, and that is normal and not a catastrophe.

4. Competence is an advantage worth striving for. But it is clearly not a requirement of nature. I can handle not being competent at some things I attempt.

5. When I say there are certain ways things should, must, or ought to be, I am trying to give orders to a world that does not obey me.

6. It would be a happier world if people and events turned out better. And when things do not turn out well I will probably feel frustrated and disappointed. But there is no requirement that the world be perfect. And there is certainly no requirement that I be miserable about being in an imperfect world.

7. Jumping to conclusions about the future is irrational. For instance, if I apply for a job and my application is rejected, it is not proof that I will never get a job in the future.

8. We can only control our effort; we can seldom control outcomes. Blaming myself for something over which I do not have complete control is self-defeating and irrational.

9. I have often responded to frustration by telling myself, "I can't stand it!" The truth is I "stood it" every single time. Remembering this will help me see frustrating events as inconvenient, maybe even painful, but not awful and horrible.

10. There will be times when I will do something stupidly. This does not mean I am and must forever be stupid. It just means I am imperfect, I did poorly this time, and I can live with this.

11. Many persons' lives improve. My past miseries do not guarantee more of the same. With some effort and self-discipline, I may be able to improve things.

12. Life is a series of events that are not always fair. Some events will bring pleasure and some will be inconvenient and painful. I can accept this.

13. Planning to avoid a problem is helpful. But, once a problem exists, resenting it and not facing it is a dangerous strategy.

14. Facing a problem does not mean I have to suffer. I can even take pride in my strength in finding a solution. This could increase my self-esteem.

15. I still respect and care about someone who is not living effectively or successfully. It is unfair and irrational for me to not give myself the same break.

16. Being happy usually requires effort and self-discipline. Even though I cannot always be successful, the very act of trying will make me happier.

17. I feel the way I think. If I avoid irrational thoughts, at worst I will experience inconvenience, regret and annoyance - not anxiety, depression and rage.

18. If something seems dangerous or threatening, I am better off if I take reasonable precautions. After that, there is no use worrying about it.

19. When people behave unfairly, it can cause unhappiness and frustration. But this is not proof that I will always have to put up with unfairness, and I can handle it without thinking it is a catastrophe.

20. I cannot judge the worth of any human being. Therefore my worth as a human being cannot be judged. So, when I attempt something, certain things may be at stake, but my worth as a human being is not one of them.

21. My happiness in life does not depend entirely on any one moment, endeavor or relationship.

22. There is no particular way anything must be.

Appendix D

Daily Boosts for Happiness

Michael R. Slavit, Ph.D., ABPP

It seems as though most individuals have a "default setting" with regard to their level of day-to-day happiness. Without any specific situations propelling their moods upward or downward, some people seem to be typically cheerful, some feel typically neutral, and some seem to feel typically a little low or "bummed out." Regardless of what your personal default setting may be, you will probably benefit from giving your mood a little boost several times per day.

Take a moment for each of the following:

1. Use the relaxation method we created in session to bring down your level of tension or enhance your feeling of relaxation.

2. take a moment to enjoy the beauty of nature (for example, the shape or color of clouds, the look of the bare branches of trees against the winter sky, the shapes of shrubs, the colors of flowers, et cetera).

3. Take a moment to enjoy humor. You may keep copies of your favorite cartoon book nearby, and to read a few until one gives you a laugh. Or, you can think of humorous situations you have witnessed or in which you have participated.

4. Take a moment to enjoy music. Sometimes you will enjoy music that is sprightly or driving. Sometimes you will enjoy music that is more flowing or melodic. Regardless of what type of music is available, do more than just recognize the music as something you like. Rather, really allow yourself to feel the effect of the music.

5. A moment of bliss (use one of your favorite Principles for Happiness).

6. Perform a random act of kindness. For example, hold a door for someone, pause to allow another driver to get into the line of traffic, et cetera.

If you can train yourself to review this short list of boosts for happiness, and to consciously and purposefully perform them, you will find yourself feeling better and happier. This will give you a sense of control over your own mental state and your life experience.

References

Barnet, Lincoln, *The Universe and Dr. Einstein*

Beck, Aaron T. *Cognitive Therapy and the Emotional Disorders*. New York: University Press.

Ehrmann, Max. *The Desiderata of Love*. New York: Crown Publishers, 1995.

Ellis, Albert and Harper, Robert. *A New Guide to Rational Living*. New York, 1975.

Hawking, Stephen, *A Brief History of Time: From The Big Bang to Black Holes*, New York: Bantam Books, 1988.

Smith, Manuel, *When I Say "No" I Feel Guilty*.

About the Author

Michael Slavit is a psychologist in private practice. He received his Bachelor's degree in Psychology at Brown University, his Master's degree in Counseling at the University of Rhode Island and his Doctorate in Counseling Psychology at the University of Texas at Austin. He is board certified in Cognitive and Behavioral Psychology by the American Board of Professional Psychology. But he considers his most important credential to be the confidence of his patients.

Dr. Slavit treats patients for a variety of issues including depression, anxiety, ADHD, unresolved grief and health/fitness/weight. He believes that not all personal problems have to be viewed as emotional disorders, but may be more appropriately seen as inevitable problems adjusting happily to a complex and demanding world. Dr. Slavit has produced over a hundred handouts and brochures to help educate his patients, and is the author of *Cure Your Money Ills: Improve Your Self-esteem through Personal Budgeting* and *Your Life: An Owner's Guide*. He has works in process, including books on embracing fitness and coping with ADHD.

Made in the USA
Monee, IL
18 April 2024

57138021R00074